The 13 Key Performance Indicators for Highly Effective Teams

Allam Ahmed, George Siantonas and Nicholas Siantonas

Greenleaf
PUBLISHING

2 0 0 8

Greenleaf Publishing Limited
Aizlewood's Mill
Nursery Street
Sheffield S3 8GG
UK
www.greenleaf-publishing.com

Printed in Great Britain on acid-free paper by Antony Rowe Ltd, Chippenham, Wiltshire.

FSC
Mixed Sources
Product group from well-managed
forests and other controlled sources
Cert no. SGS-COC-2953
www.fsc.org
© 1996 Forest Stewardship Council

Cover by LaliAbril.com

British Library Cataloguing in Publication Data:

Ahmed, Allam
   The 13 key performance indicators for highly effective
   teams
   1. Teams in the workplace - Evaluation
   I. Title II. Siantonas, George III. Siantonas, Nicholas
   IV. The thirteen key peirformance indicators for highly
   effective teams
   658.4'022

ISBN-13: 9781906093075

Contents

List of figures and tables

FIGURES

TABLES

Acknowledgements

We would like to thank a number of colleagues whose advice and ideas have contributed to this book.

Dr Kkalid Alrawi, Al-Ain University of Science and Technology, UAE, for his invaluable contribution and helpful notes.

Liz Bennett, SIA Managing Consultant, and Andy Webber, SIA Principal Consultant, whose creativity, innovation and professionalism have played a significant part in the development of the TPD and its application in many organisations in the UK and globally. Eddie Winton, SIA Principal Consultant, and Michelle Crouch, The Source—Marketing Consultancy, for their patient work in assisting in the proofreading of the statistical analysis. Finally, the whole team at SIA, who constantly demonstrate the 13 Key Performance Indicators of a highly effective team.

We would like also to thank Greenleaf Publishing and most sincerely John Stuart and Dean Bargh and their highly professional staff for giving us the opportunity to publish this book in such a short time.

Allam, George and Nick
Brighton, November 2007

1

Aims and methodology

Introduction

While many organisations are great at managing the materials and machinery, they often fall very short in being able to manage the human side of their business. If members of the organisation don't take personal responsibility for their own actions, decisions and results, then they won't be able to build trust. Teams are defined by many scholars as a small number of people with complementary skills who are committed to a common purpose, performance goals and approach for which they hold themselves mutually accountable (see Huczynski and Buchanan 2006; Dixon 1991; Drucker 1998; Ghoshal *et al.* 2003; Hofstede 1991; Needle 2001; Kraft 1999; Michalski and King 1998; among others). These skills include being a team player, a propensity for participation, cooperative behaviour and leadership.

Essentially, there are two major issues to consider when people come together in a work group or team within an organisation.

- The first issue—and frequently this is the only one the group considers—is the task and the problems involved in getting the job done

- The second issue—and the one least often considered by the group/team—is the process of the group work itself: the mechanisms by which the group acts as a unit and not as a loose rabble

Without due attention to this latter process, the value of the group and human capital of the organisation can be diminished or even destroyed.

Effective explicit management of this process can enhance the worth of the group to a point where it is many times the sum of the worth of its individuals. This then leads to synergy, which in turn engenders a positive organisational culture and makes group work attractive in organisations despite the possible problems of (and time spent in) group formation.

The right degree of knowledge, skill and attitude are essential ingredients for high performance in all fields of human endeavour. However, if a goal can be reached only when people work together in a team, their individual talents alone are not enough. What matters most is the intangible element often referred to as *chemistry* or the extent to which people *gel together*.

SIA Group

SIA Group was established in 1982, since which time it has gained an international reputation for the design and delivery of programmes that equip people with the knowledge, experiences and skills they need to excel in the workplace and improve people performance. For many years, SIA Group has delivered its programmes and training for over 100 organisations worldwide ranging from multinational enterprises to smaller companies and government organisations.[1]

SIA Group's work has resulted in the creation of a unique, new and electronically administered Team Performance Diagnostic (TPD) tool. The tool enables functional heads and managers to quickly gain an accurate and detailed insight into the real-life functioning and 'health' of their current team. TPD helps managers to:

- Understand team dynamics
- Enhance team sprit
- Encourage communication
- Identify development activities
- Maximise team performance
- Allocate training budgets effectively
- Quickly reach higher levels of team performance

To date, the tool has been extensively used in major multinational and UK public sector organisations to pinpoint those hard-to-find opportunities to achieve rapid improvements. The key advantages of TPD are:

---

1 More information about SIA Group is available at www.siagroup.co.uk.

- Improve results and reach higher levels of team performance

- Quickly establish how to generate fast improvements in team effectiveness

- Undertake development activities that maximise team performance

Objectives

Based on SIA's TPD tool, this study aims to contribute to the understanding of the nature and functioning of teamwork cohesiveness in organisations at different levels by describing teamwork as a multi-component variable and identifying the factors that operate in combination when teamwork is taking place, and examining the implications of teamwork for the effectiveness of the organisation. It also aims to expand the knowledge and understanding of sourcing team interaction and effectiveness.

The main objective is to identify the most current trends of team effectiveness across as wide a range of sectors as possible within the United Kingdom. The researchers have worked to capture a snapshot from data across a range of industry sectors to make it possible to pull out any trends that are running within a specific industry. This enabled the researchers to explore the aggregate analysis of survey results and an analysis of the sector as a whole.

Methodology

The research method used for this study is based on the work that has been undertaken by SIA Group over the last 26 years in helping clients to achieve more with and through their teams. This extensive work has now been captured to identify 13 Key Performance Indicators (see Appendix 1), which serve as drivers or 'team health' indicators.

Building on a comprehensive review of the relevant literature, the secondary data collection focused on the derivation of appropriate testable hypotheses linked to the research objectives above. A number of key databases were used to extract published and comparative data focusing on organisational culture, motivation and group dynamics, among others.

The primary data was collected from different industry sectors in the UK in the period 15 May to 20 July 2006. During the study, time was allocated for checking and clarifying the completed questionnaires, correcting any information or descriptions while the details could still be clearly remembered, as well as gathering all relevant literature. After incorporating corrections, six researchers were interviewed for pre-testing of the questionnaire.

The final version of the questionnaire, which consists of 156 questions across the 13 key team performance indicators, was then produced accordingly and data was gathered from the different sectors as designated.

Data collection

An email invitation was sent out to a selection of human resources (HR), training/learning professionals and managers on the SIA prospects database comprising 693 contacts from which a total of 81 responses were received.

The email invitation contains information about the aims of the national team performance perception survey, an incentive to complete the survey (win a bottle of champagne and free copy of the final report) and a link to our online survey/questionnaire (see Appendix 2).

The online questionnaire was designed by selecting the 13 key team performance indicators as featured in the TPD tool to focus on personal perception only across these 13 team performance indicators. The other advantages of the online questionnaire are that it allowed us to collate all responses in electronic format to populate our sector, and provided indicator spreadsheets for quick reporting—and consequently providing data for the output of aggregated graphs and stats for each sector and team performance indicator.

The questionnaire was completed on a fully anonymous basis, enabling participants to be entirely honest in their responses, expressing their own views and opinions confidentially.

All contacts in the database represent nine sectors/industries, encompassing small, medium and large organisations: education; electronics and technology; finance and insurance; healthcare; local government; professional services; retail; telecommunications; and travel and leisure. The sector 'professional services' includes companies in the fields of recruitment, consultancy, business solutions and website construction.

Finally, the results of the diagnosis are incorporated in a comprehensive colour report with up to 25 pages of in-depth analysis presented in the form of coloured bar charts, data tables and narrative (see Appendix 3 for a sample TPD report). This data is presented by an SIA Group consultant, to advise on individual and team development plans and decision-making.

2

Concept and theory

Introduction

Researchers have long been interested in the study of teamwork in organisations, as fostering teamwork is a top priority for many leaders (Nelson 1995). The benefits are clear: increased productivity, improved customer service, a more flexible system and employee empowerment.

For the purpose of this study, several sources have been consulted, including refereed journals, online databases and governmental reports and statistics. However, it is clear from the outset that there are limitations on the availability of literature specifically focusing on UK team effectiveness. The literature on teamwork has been dominated by issues relating to interpersonal work relationship, governance structures or even societies as a whole. It is therefore important at the start of this chapter to explore several conceptual issues relating to organisational culture, motivation and group dynamics.

Organisation and culture

There are several definitions of an organisation but, in simple terms, an organisation is defined by Haberberg and Reiple (2001) as a social system with an economic purpose. This social system includes a group of people, an economic actor, an accumulation of knowledge and learning as well as a bundle of resources. Therefore, no analysis is complete unless it takes account of all these aspects at once.

Organisations have to be managed to provide a cohesive structure for their daily operations. An organisation's most important asset is its people. Everyone is seeking to achieve many different things from the collective purposes of the organisation rather than the goods and services it provides. The employees look to their organisation not only as a source of money but also as a source of meaning, stability, security, support, protection, self-esteem, self-confidence, power and control, among other things (Huczynski and Buchanan 2006). People at work are motivated by more than just pay and conditions; their need for recognition and a sense of belonging are very important (Bozeman and Straussman 1990). Human beings have reasons for the things that they do and our behaviour is actually purposive (Maslow 1970). Everything may be more productive *if* your people are sufficiently motivated, trained, informed, managed, utilised and empowered (McLagan 1989).

The human experience is one of cultures. Culture and cultural differences have been at the heart of human behaviour throughout history. Indeed, at the end of the 20th century, the significance of culture was highlighted in the rethinking of world politics that stemmed from the end of the Cold War and the increasing pace of globalisation. The shrinking of the globe brought different cultures into closer contact and represented a challenge to traditional patterns of culture and social order.

People faced the dilemma of what in their cultures could be maintained and what would be lost. Cultural change created friction. When people of one culture perceive those of another not just as alien, but also as threatening, conflict is likely. Long-suppressed cultural conflicts reignited following the Cold War. Peoples clashed at a local level but there was also a broader tension between global and local forces. The culture of the West was the dominant force in globalisation, and, while Western culture seemed to be making the human experience more homogeneous, it was also prompting cultural counter-reactions.

Many writers (e.g. Ghoshal *et al.* 2003; Johnson *et al.* 2005; Lynch 2003) have attempted to define culture in different ways, but almost all of them agree on the broad definition of culture as a body of learned behaviour, a collection of beliefs, habits and traditions, shared by a group of people and successively learned by people who enter society. However, most notable is Hofstede's (1994) definition of culture as *'the collective programming of the mind, which distinguishes the members of one group or category of people from another'*. Generally speaking, the public sector environment is complex.

Culture comprises ideas through which we perceive and interpret the world, symbols we use to communicate these ideas, and institutions, which enable individuals to become members of society and satisfy their needs. At its most visible it represents those goods and institutions that most readily distinguish one culture from another, such as architecture, food, ceremonies, language, and the different emphasis placed by different cultures on aspects of the educational system. Culture comprises our notions of 'right' and 'wrong', our norms, our notions about what is 'good' and 'bad', our values and things we hold to be true—our beliefs.

Many problems associated with the relationships between people of different cultures stem from variations in norms, values and beliefs. At its deepest level, however, culture comprises a set of basic assumptions that operate automatically to enable groups of people to solve the problems of daily life without thinking about them. In this way, culture is that which causes one group of people to act collectively in a way that is different from another group of people. We often tend to equate culture with nationality. While most nation-states have their own national cultural characteristics, some countries are typified by two or more cultural groups. Each of these groups has its own customs and behaviour.

Group dynamics

Any person's attitude to work is shaped strongly by the group to which that individual belongs within the institution. The ability of the informal group to motivate an individual at work should not be underestimated (Pettinger 2001). Working in groups is one of the main activities of institution-wide quality improvement, but when handled poorly it can be time-consuming, frustrating and ineffective. However, when groups work well, it can be a stimulating and rewarding experience. We are not all naturally good at working together but, although it is not an easy process, there are ways in which the institution's directors can improve the effectiveness of groups and teams. They can also, as outsiders, help groups by being an effective facilitator for them.

An effective team would have clear, cooperative goals to which every team member is committed; accurate and effective communication of ideas and feelings; distributed participation and leadership; appropriate and effective decision-making procedures; productive controversies; a high level of trust, acceptance and support among members; a high level of cohesion; constructive management of power and conflict; and adequate problem-solving procedures (see Hughes 1998; Joyce 1999; Pettinger 2001). An effective team has clear benefits for the institution, the individual team members and, importantly, for their clients.

When individuals come together in teams, their differences in terms of power, values and attitudes contribute to the creation of conflict. As a result, an enormous variety of approaches and definitions have emerged across disciplines, appearing sometimes to ignore each other's contributions; therefore most methods of resolving conflict stress the importance of dealing with disputes quickly and openly (Thamhain and Wilemon 1975). Conflict is not necessarily destructive, however; when managed properly, conflict can result in benefits for the team. Recognising that teamwork reflects a multitude of roles, teams will need to face up to the downside of greater empowerment; therefore functions and levels of analysis have been a turning point for theory and research on this topic.

Management also needs to define the role of team leadership. Although members can share or rotate leadership responsibility, the individual(s) assuming formal leadership must understand the requirements of the position. Clear boundaries for the trust concept are necessary in order to understand what is meant by teamwork and how to define it. As a consequence, the bedrock of traditional hierarchy is being relentlessly undermined in the process. So thoughtful organisations will inevitably feel the need to change the way their managers approach their jobs.

An effective leader must maintain a team's focus on its assignment while establishing positive relations with team members. It is very important for team members to have common goals for team achievement, as well as to communicate clearly about the individual goals that they may have. Indeed, sharing goals is one of the definitional properties of the concept of 'team'. A simple, but useful, team-building task is to assign a newly formed team the task of producing a mission and goals statement. For any real value to be gained from teamwork development initiatives, organisations must be able to get members to recognise a whole range of contributions made by different team members. Only then will they be able to think about how best they can exploit this potential and work effectively together to ensure that everyone plays to his/her strengths and maximises the team's effort.

Teamwork building and concept

Team formation involves a number of critical decisions. This includes selecting the right teamwork members, identifying the functions required to support a team's assignment, and determining the team's size. However, in defining teamwork, several factors are noted, such as: everyone in the team is expected to participate actively and positively in the team meetings and projects; he/she trusts the judgement of others; members are carefully listened to and receive thoughtful feedback; and the team is willing to take risks (Yarbrough 2002; Hersey *et al.* 2001).

Team members should develop different patterns of communication and interaction which influence how well the team works together. Assessing and planning now give way to team interaction and participation. Successful interaction depends largely on an organisation's ability to promote member effort and a team's ability to develop appropriate team performance strategies.

The process of manpower planning and control is concerned with matching future manpower requirements with future manpower availability, and involves considerations of both the quantity and the quality of the labour force, including the analysis of such factors as the age profile of the staff (see Needle 2001: 450).

In most definitions, teamwork appears related to a small number of people with complementary skills who are committed to a common purpose, performance goals and approach for which they hold themselves mutually accountable (Kraft 1999). For Michalski and King (1998), all teams are groups of individuals but not all groups of individuals necessarily demonstrate the cohesiveness of a team. Teams outperform individuals because teams generate a special energy. This energy develops as team members work together fusing their personal energies and talents to deliver tangible performance results.

Working together as teams to establish specific performance objectives helps transform a team from a group of individuals into a committed group. Before a team begins formal work on its assignment, it is critical that executive management clarify the reason for the team's existence. Furthermore, team members must understand how management expects them to support the team and why they were selected as members. The willingness to take risks (Tepper *et al.* 2001) is one of the definitions of teamwork and has played a role in many conceptualisations. The idea of being vulnerable as a leader or a team member conjures up images of weakness and ineptitude. For instance, Osborn and Moran (2000) refer to teamwork as the concept of people working together cooperatively in the organisation. We often see vulnerability as a weakness, but we forget that, when a person is vulnerable in the sense that he/she is open to criticism, he/she is in fact exceptionally strong. Having the courage to face candid feedback takes great strength; this confidence tends to be found only in people who possess sufficient self-belief to weigh up the value of any criticism levelled against them. However, for Luhmann (1979), risk is a prerequisite in the choice to trust. The reverse of this often manifests itself in managers or leaders who avoid candid feedback by pronouncing their own opinions with such vigour that no one else would dare to question them. In doing this they immediately weaken the team, as decisions can be made only from the top without drawing on the views, experiences and opinions of those they are working with. Effective managers are able to combine the need for decisive, clear and confident direction with openness and accessibility. They also appreciate that authority comes as much from asking the right questions as from giving the right answers.

Teamwork is also contingent on a certain situation and tends to be based not only on personal information but also on non-personal information. LaFasto and Larson (2001) argue that teamwork involves not only reinforcing individual capabilities but also creating participation and involvement, distributing the workload and generating a diversity of ideas. Teams have become the latest obsession for managers, who are now striving to set up efficient teamwork procedures in their organisations.

According to Zhou and George (2001), high-performance teams do not appear spontaneously. They are grown, nurtured and exercised. It takes a lot of hard work and skill to blend different personalities, abilities and visionary leader. A leader whose job is not to control, but to teach, encourages, and organises when necessary.

Throughout the literature review, a variety of behaviours has appeared indicative of teamwork, including interdependence (Rousseau 2001), goal specification (Besser 1995), cohesiveness (Latham 2001), roles and norms (VandeWalle *et al.* 2001), communication (Clampitt *et al.* 2000) and trust (Bryant and Harvey 2000). The relative importance of each form of behaviour depends on the nature and context of the work relationship. Interdependence is the issue of how each member's outcomes are determined, at least in part, by the actions of the other members. Functioning independently of other team members or competing with them should lead to suboptimal outcomes for the entire team. Effective interpersonal communication is vital to the smooth functioning of any task team. Every team has to develop an effective communication network. Norms will develop governing communication (Baron and Byrne 1991).

Goal specification and cohesiveness refers to the attractiveness of team membership. In task-oriented teams the concept can be differentiated into two sub-concepts: social cohesiveness and task cohesiveness. Social cohesiveness refers to the bonds of interpersonal attraction that link team members. Nevertheless, the patterns of interpersonal attraction within a team are a very prominent concern. Task cohesiveness refers to the way in which skills and abilities of the team members mesh to allow effective performance (Arthur and Aiman-Smith 2001).

Moreover, it is very important that team goals are understood by everyone and all members are carefully listened to and receive thoughtful feedback. Everyone should be supportive of the project and of others; it is essential that the role structure enables the team to cope effectively with the requirements of the task, and the assignment of roles to members who can perform them effectively is essential (Avolio 1999).

Trust is difficult to create in a competitive environment—and most companies provide a competitive environment. One of the problems with solving a trust issue is that the manager never knows what the underlying issues are if people are not willing to share them. This is often the case, particularly in a multi-person setting. Even if trust exists and team members are willing to engage in constructive conflict, some people will naturally try to avoid conflict at all costs. Team members have to trust the people and process, and team members have to be willing to contribute to team debates; in other words, they have to be willing to engage in constructive conflict on the work itself (Smith 1999).

In line with several of these multidimensional conceptualisations of teamwork, we propose that teamwork is not only a psychological state based on expectations and on perceived motives and intentions of others, but also a manifestation of behaviour towards others (Costa *et al.* 2001).

Evaluating teamwork effectiveness

Understanding each other is essential for teamwork. The critical point is to understand the weaknesses and strengths of each member. The issue is how to reveal the potential abilities of members, how to actualise their power, and how to use these to add to team strengths and compensate for team weaknesses. Amabile (1998) argues that, when team members compete with each other, disclosing weaknesses and nullifying strengths in the process, teamwork ends and the cause is ruined. Researchers usually assess effectiveness in teamwork by the mutual respect of others' values and standards. Every member holds distinct values and standards. These are not ways of criticising others, or pigeonholing them. All values and standards are useful in a colourful and dynamic organisation. Good teamwork always elevates members, enhancing and complementing their personalities and their abilities (Meyerson 2001).

Certainly, when organisations implement teamwork well, then unity is aspired to and individuals don't feel the need to advance their own interests. Greg *et al.* (1999) identify a positive relation between the availability of certain organisational resources and effective team leadership. However, individuals or groups that want to influence members of organisations in this fashion are used to using the words 'unity' and 'stability of organisation' to their own advantage. Teamwork, on the other hand, is a collective leadership system. The aim or goals of an organisation are undertaken by all members and do not depend on a single person or group.

The building of unity in a team of individuals will be crucial to the success of the organisation. If unity is disrupted by discordant relationships, a team will not accomplish its goals. Carrie (1985) examines a number of organisational benefits that can result from the successful use of sourcing teamwork, and the highest perceived benefit is found to be the ability to bring greater knowledge and skill together at one time. A solid cooperative team can create an environment for learning, serving and growing together. William (1999) argues that creating a team whose members have heterogeneous skills, backgrounds and experiences increases the probability that each member can contribute the knowledge and skill required to support sourcing team assignments. Unique contributions by individual members, in turn, increase the likelihood that a team will benefit from dynamic cross-functional interaction.

One explanation can be related to the fact that, in most empirical studies, teamwork has been conceptualised as a psychological state, such as belief or an attitude towards a known individual or group of individuals, in opposition to teamwork as a multidimensional or multi-component construct.

The problem in clarifying the reality of high-performance teamwork is trying to find consensus about what it is. Researchers of the phenomenon use various phrases to describe its features: intelligence and skills, self-managed teams, merit and performance. However, the most common characteristics (Baron *et al.* 2007; Galagan 1994) appear to be collaboration among teams, between employee and management.

Managers in today's organisations are under intense pressure to improve performance across multiple perspectives: cost controls and financial reporting, value creation and information access, employee productivity, customer satisfaction, and long-term strategic partnerships. Therefore organisations must determine what performance capabilities and outcomes they need. Performance is defined as realising specific outcomes through managing organisational portfolios of people, processes and programmes (White 1994). The qualities demanded of high-performance workers—the ability to create, extend and apply knowledge, sophisticated skills, adaptability and flexibility, change management, the ability to work in teams of diverse people—are also those needed to solve the economic and social problems they raise. Stewart (1993) argues that teamworkers therefore have the best understanding of how well their team performs tasks in relation to their objectives. Although the benefits of team performance may not yet be tangible, doing nothing to prepare workers for teamwork seems the best way to ensure that the benefits remain unrealised. The most important goal of team cohesiveness is to improve performance in the future and not just for the employee. Work units and organisations can identify problems that interfere with everyone's work. Therefore, we can expect a positive relation between cohesiveness within teamwork and task performance.

3

Industry aggregate analysis

Introduction

In this chapter we will explore the aggregate analysis of survey results and an analysis of the industry as a whole. However, in the next chapter the results will be discussed in greater detail broken down by industry sector.

Figure 1 shows the overall average for all industries in each of the 13 indicator categories (see Box 1; see also Appendix 1). Figure 1 is useful to the extent that it reveals 'universal' trends that may emerge within all teams regardless of industry sector. It can be used to analyse whether there are any UK-wide 'development' areas or 'maintain and build' areas.

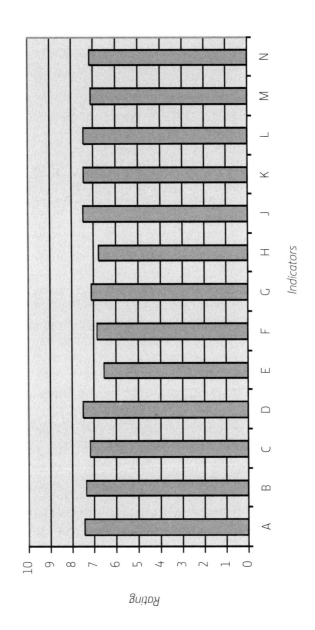

FIGURE 1 Survey average

A   Balanced roles
B   Clear objectives and purpose
C   Openness, trust, confrontation and conflict resolution
D   Cooperation, support, interpersonal communication and relationships
E   Individual and team learning and development
F   Sound inter-group relations and communications
G   Appropriate management/leadership
H   Sound team procedures and regular review
J   Output, performance, quality and accountability
K   Morale
L   Empowerment
M   Change, creativity and challenging the status quo
N   Decision-making and problem-solving

Box 1   The 13 Key Performance Indicators

The graph shows that indicator E has the lowest-scoring average (6.53); this indicator represents *Individual and team learning and development*. It is a mid-range score, highlighting an area for improvement but not of urgent concern. A score of this level in this area may indicate learning and development needs to be addressed more effectively at both an individual and a team level, or there could be an imbalance between the two. There may not be enough training and learning opportunities available, and these may not be the most appropriate ones. Needs may not be addressed in a timely manner. The quality of learning and development activities offered to individuals and the team could be improved and more could be done to develop the team as a whole, in particular ensuring that the various members work together even more effectively. All of these points would be explored in a Team Performance Diagnostic (TPD) and it would be possible to identify the specific contributing factors and plan appropriate improvement actions to resolve the issues.

However, as with any aggregation, this 'top level' view is of limited value. The results range from a high of 7.48 (D) to a low of 6.53 (E); a very small spectrum of around 1. Unsurprisingly, this has occurred because the responses are from a number of different industries and this masks any industry trends that may be emerging; for example, the fact that the scores for *Morale*—indicator K—from the telecommunications sector are lower than all the other sectors in the survey may be as a result of the restructuring in the sector over the last five years. Conversely, the introduction of low-cost airlines into the travel and leisure market, coupled with the fact that people around the world have more disposable income than ever before, may have caused a boost in morale and 'excitement' within organisations in this industry. These two opposing scores lead to a cancelling-out effect, and thus the indicator for *Morale*, like all indicators, remains within this small range.

Figure 2 shows the same survey data as in Figure 1—this time plotted against the average responses from the Team Performance Diagnostic database. These results consist of the average responses in each indicator of every team that completed a full TPD. The same problem of levelling of results due to opposing scoring, identified earlier, applies; however, the TPD results are much more indicative of universal team trends. This is because team members contributing to a full TPD are asked to complete a far more extensive and complex questionnaire. Owing to this, and the fact that the TPD database holds a larger sample size, it can be assumed that these results make for a more accurate representation of the actual population than the survey responses.

Moreover, in Figure 3, the range of the TPD data is much greater, peaking at a high of 8 for indicators G and L and slumping to a low of 5.5 for indicator H, a total range of 3.5 compared with a range of 1 for the survey responses. Therefore, taking these results to be more accurate of universal issues (i.e. independent of industry), it is possible to pick out some emerging patterns.

Indicators F and H—which represent *Sound inter-group relations and communications* and *Sound team procedures and regular review*, respectively—seem to be universal development areas with scores of 5.7 and 5.5 respectively.

At the other end of the scale, indicator G (*Appropriate management/leadership*) and indicator L (*Empowerment*) score very highly at an average of 8 each. This suggests that nationwide the style of leadership and management displayed within teams is likely to be contributing positively towards how motivated and empowered the teams are feeling. There is a good balance between the amount of support and direction provided to teams. The nature of support and direction is also likely to be good. Communication and feedback between management, individuals and their teams as a whole are appropriate in terms of both quality and quantity. Team members also have the resources they need to enable them to carry out their roles. They feel that they have appropriate freedom to make and implement decisions within the remit of their role. There is a good balance between providing direction/supervision and allowing individuals the freedom to act and to genuinely feel empowered. Team members also feel that opportunities exist to contribute towards wider decisions that affect the whole team. The members of this team generally feel well consulted.

A possible reason behind this pattern may be that empowerment in the workplace has grown ever more important within organisations over the last 20 years. The idea of

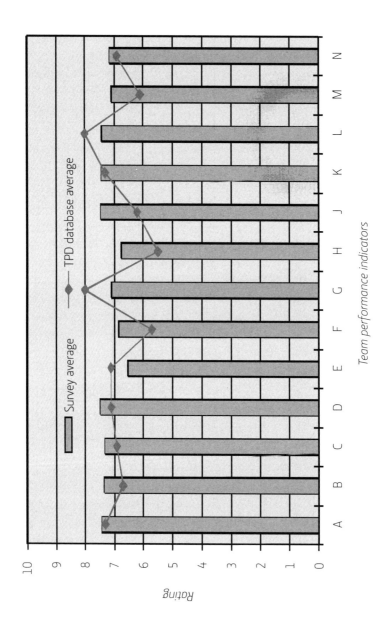

FIGURE 2 Survey average versus TPD database average

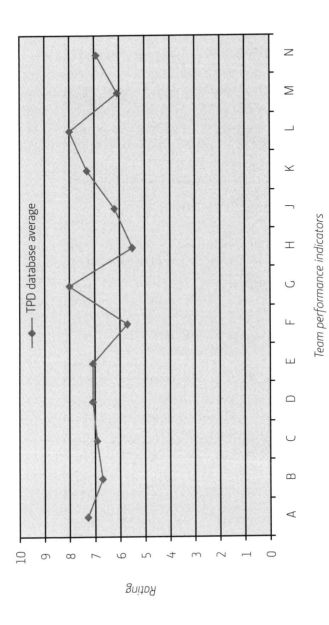

FIGURE 3 **TPD database average**

empowering individual workers and giving them greater scope for self-management and responsibility has been a major element in many organisational training programmes. During the mid to late '80s the Thatcher government began to 'roll back the state' in a bid to create a more efficient business environment. Not only did this involve privatisation but it also saw a cutback in industry bureaucracy, leading to smaller and 'quicker' workforces. This meant that individual workers no longer had a large—and sometimes bureaucratic—structure in place to support them; as a consequence, there was a drive within many organisations to empower workers and make them more self-reliant. Empowerment has been a management and training mantra for a long time now, and it may well be that it is now more embedded within the cultures of many organisations than previously was the case.

Industry analysis

This section breaks down the specific industry trends within the nine sectors surveyed. These nine industries are: education; electronics and technology; finance and insurance; healthcare; local government; professional services; retail; telecommunications; and travel and leisure. The sector 'professional services' includes companies in the fields of recruitment, consultancy, business solutions and website construction. The breakdown of the industry sectors within the survey data is shown in Figure 4.

Figure 5 and Table 1 show the average survey response from the nine different sectors. While the graph is challenging to interpret, it is noticeable that five of the nine industries shown follow a very similar pattern.

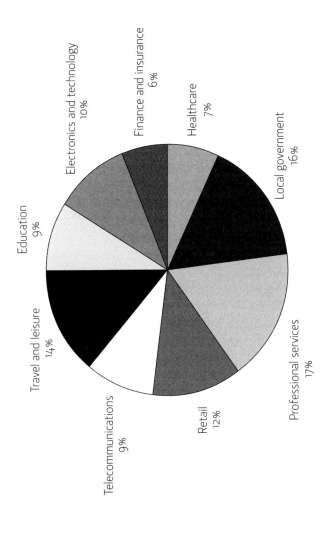

FIGURE 4 **Breakdown of industry sectors**

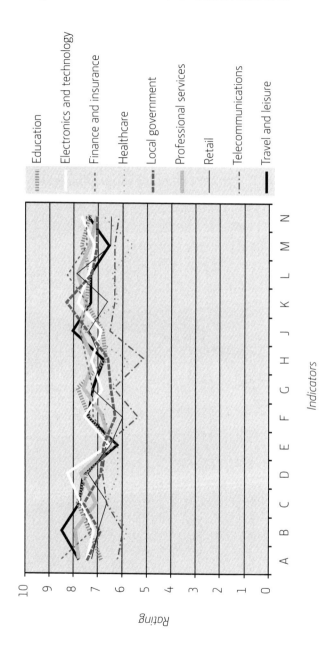

FIGURE 5 **Industry analysis**

	A	B	C	D	E	F	G	H	J	K	L	M	N
Education	6.83	7.33	7.83	7.50	6.50	7.33	7.83	6.67	6.83	7.50	7.33	7.67	7.33
Electronics and technology	7.43	7.14	7.71	8.29	6.57	7.57	6.86	7.29	6.86	7.86	7.43	7.14	7.71
Finance and insurance	8.50	7.25	7.75	7.50	6.25	7.25	7.25	7.50	7.75	7.50	8.25	7.50	7.50
Healthcare	6.20	5.80	6.60	6.20	6.20	6.80	6.40	5.80	7.60	6.20	6.40	5.60	6.80
Local government	7.40	6.90	7.60	6.90	6.80	6.30	6.50	6.60	7.40	8.30	7.30	7.10	7.10
Professional services	7.75	7.92	7.08	7.67	6.50	6.83	7.58	7.17	7.75	7.50	7.83	7.33	7.08
Retail	7.25	7.00	6.63	7.38	6.50	6.00	7.25	6.88	7.38	6.63	7.88	6.50	6.50
Telecommunications	6.17	6.00	6.67	6.83	6.67	5.33	6.33	5.17	6.50	6.33	6.33	6.33	6.17
Travel and leisure	7.80	8.50	7.80	7.60	6.20	7.40	7.20	6.80	8.00	7.30	7.30	6.60	7.40
Average	7.43	7.35	7.35	7.48	6.53	6.83	7.09	6.75	7.46	7.43	7.42	7.09	7.15

TABLE 1 Industry analysis

Figure 6 shows five sectors—education; electronics and technology; finance and insurance; professional services; and travel and leisure—plotted against the average of all the survey data.

The average responses for each of the five industry sectors very closely matches the overall survey average, indicating there to be at least a semblance of a national trend among teams, irrespective of industry sector. This is especially obvious in the case of indicator E— *Individual and team learning and development*—where all five industry sectors score at a similarly low level, which also matches the overall average score (this is highlighted in Table 2).

Of the whole survey, the five sectors account for only 48% of responses. This discounts the possibility the result is being unevenly skewed by these industry sectors comprising most of the survey responses; the data indicates that *Individual and team learning and development* is an issue facing teams in general, whatever the industry sector. This is further evidenced by the fact that this indicator had by far the lowest spread of scores from all nine sectors (0.60 variation, with the next lowest variation being 1.23 and many in excess of 2.00).

There could be a number of reasons why this indicator is performing badly in comparison with the others.

- Greater expectations from team members about the sort of opportunities there should be

- Reliance on the organisation rather than team leader/ manager providing training

- A mind-set that sees learning and development as a cost rather than an investment

- Failure to follow up learning activities in the workplace

- Uninspired previous training experiences
- Cyclical swings in the amount of learning and development provided
- The amount of change taking place which makes it difficult for team members to believe they are keeping up with it all

Clearly there needs to be greater emphasis on identifying which are the relevant factors for any particular team in a given industry before the situation can be properly addressed.

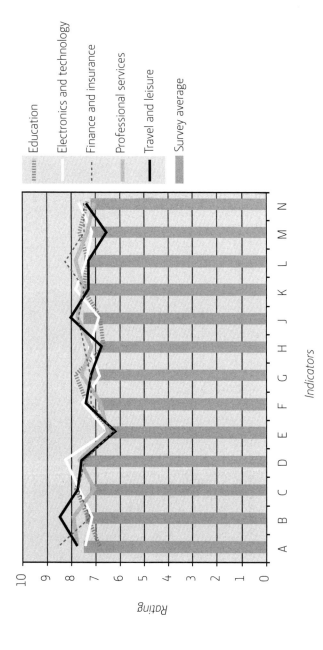

FIGURE 6 Industry analysis: five selected sectors

	A	B	C	D	E	F	G	H	J	K	L	M	N
Education	6.83	7.33	7.83	7.50	6.50	7.33	7.83	6.67	6.83	7.50	7.33	7.67	7.33
Electronics and technology	7.43	7.14	7.71	8.29	6.57	7.57	6.86	7.29	6.86	7.86	7.43	7.14	7.71
Finance and insurance	8.50	7.25	7.75	7.50	6.25	7.25	7.25	7.50	7.75	7.50	8.25	7.50	7.50
Professional services	7.75	7.92	7.08	7.67	6.50	6.83	7.58	7.17	7.75	7.50	7.83	7.33	7.08
Travel and leisure	7.80	8.50	7.80	7.60	6.20	7.40	7.20	6.80	8.00	7.30	7.30	6.60	7.40
Average	7.43	7.35	7.48		6.53	6.83	7.09	6.75	7.46	7.43	7.42	7.09	7.15

Table 2 Industry analysis: five selected sectors, highlighting *Individual and team learning and development*

Industry sector analysis

Introduction

In this chapter, the results of the in-depth analysis are presented in the form of bar charts, data tables and narrative for all industry sectors, each one in turn.

Telecommunications

Table 3 and Figure 7 show the survey average data plotted against the average for the telecommunications industry. The ratings for the telecommunications industry in 12 out of the 13 indicators are significantly lower than those of the average results, with E (*Individual and team learning and development*) being

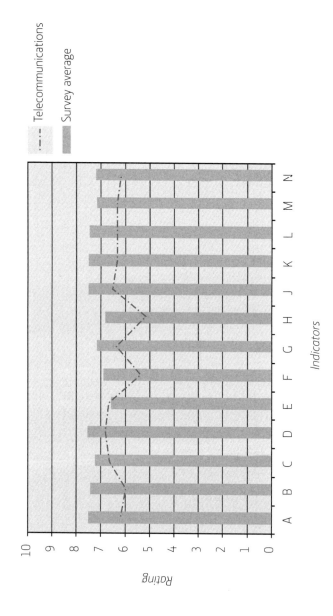

FIGURE 7 Survey average data plotted against the average for the telecommunications industry

	A	B	C	D	E	F	G	H	J	K	L	M	N
Education	6.83	7.33	7.83	7.50	6.50	7.33	7.83	6.67	6.83	7.50	7.33	7.67	7.33
Electronics and technology	7.43	7.14	7.71	8.29	6.57	7.57	6.86	7.29	6.86	7.86	7.43	7.14	7.71
Finance and insurance	8.50	7.25	7.75	7.50	6.25	7.25	7.25	7.50	7.75	7.50	8.25	7.50	7.50
Healthcare	6.20	5.80	6.60	6.20	6.20	6.80	6.40	5.80	7.60	6.20	6.40	5.60	6.80
Local government	7.40	6.90	7.60	6.90	6.80	6.30	6.50	6.60	7.40	8.30	7.30	7.10	7.10
Professional services	7.75	7.92	7.08	7.67	6.50	6.83	7.58	7.17	7.75	7.50	7.83	7.33	7.08
Retail	7.25	7.00	6.63	7.38	6.50	6.00	7.25	6.88	7.38	6.63	7.88	6.50	6.50
Telecommunications	6.17	6.00	6.67	6.83	6.67	5.33	6.33	5.17	6.50	6.33	6.33	6.33	6.17
Travel and leisure	7.80	8.50	7.80	7.60	6.20	7.40	7.20	6.80	8.00	7.30	7.30	6.60	7.40
Average	7.43	7.35	7.35	7.48	6.53	6.83	7.09	6.75	7.46	7.43	7.42	7.09	7.15

TABLE 3 Survey average data plotted against the average for the telecommunications industry

the only exception. The indicators representing *Sound inter-group relations and communications* (F) and *Sound team procedures and regular review* (H) are particularly low.

The notion of 'Sound inter-group relations and communications' is based around having a well-organised and efficient team that works together well and can effectively communicate the direction, results and output of the team. If the team scores low in this area, it is an indication that relationships and communication channels between this team and other parts of the organisation may be questionable. Individuals and teams from other departments may not view the team entirely positively, or views may be mixed. The team may feel isolated from other parts of the organisation, not knowing what some other people do, or even who they are. These issues may extend to working relationships and communications with some external customers. There may be a lack of effective cross-team working relationships and communications.

Sound team procedures and regular review (H) in this industry has a score of 5.17, which is a long way below the average for all industries of 6.75 (see Table 3 for details). This is indicative that current team processes and procedures could benefit from a thorough review. Some, rather than helping, may actually be felt to be hindering the effectiveness of the team. It may be that some less value-adding processes can be eliminated or at least streamlined. Perhaps long-established processes have simply not been modified in response to changing circumstances. There could also be improvements in the way in which the team reviews its work.

These results are interesting and may well be linked to the restructuring that the telecommunications industry has undergone in recent years. Rapid growth in the late '90s due to the boom in demand for mobile phones led to excess supply and therefore consistent price deflation in the early '00s. The infrastructure of the industry is changing too. In recent years, with the birth of wireless internet access, there has been a move away from wired and wireless transmission of audio—i.e. mobile phones only—and towards 3G. The geographic profile of the industry is also changing. The rapid growth of the 'Asian tiger economies' has meant a substantial number of people now have enough disposable income to become mobile phone and internet users. China is predicted to be the largest 'mobile market' by 2010.

All these changes have meant that the internal structures of most telecommunications organisations have changed regularly over the last few years. The price deflation in the early '00s led to large redundancies in a bid to cut costs, resulting in very low morale and poor inter-group communications because team members would be constantly changed. This may have led to neglect in the areas of team procedures and regular review. Owing to industrial and geographical reshaping in the most recent years, new teams have had to be formed to deal with these new challenges. These new teams may not yet have structures in place to carry out regular reviews, or perhaps the old ones are not relevant in the current industry climate. These new teams may not have had the time to produce substantial results, thus attracting scepticism from other groups in the organisation; this may account for the low score concerning sound inter-group relations.

Retail

Table 4 and Figure 8 show the average results for the retail industry against the survey average. They tend to mirror the survey average, dropping to a low of 6 for indicator F, *Sound inter-group relations and communications*, and peaking at a high of 7.88 for indicator L, *Empowerment*.

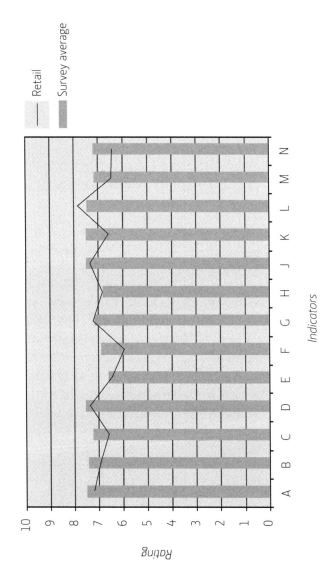

FIGURE 8 Survey average data plotted against the average for the retail industry

	A	B	C	D	E	F	G	H	J	K	L	M	N
Education	6.83	7.33	7.83	7.50	6.50	7.33	7.83	6.67	6.83	7.50	7.33	7.67	7.33
Electronics and technology	7.43	7.14	7.71	8.29	6.57	7.57	6.86	7.29	6.86	7.86	7.43	7.14	7.71
Finance and insurance	8.50	7.25	7.75	7.50	6.25	7.25	7.25	7.50	7.75	7.50	8.25	7.50	7.50
Healthcare	6.20	5.80	6.60	6.20	6.20	6.80	6.40	5.80	7.60	6.20	6.40	5.60	6.80
Local government	7.40	6.90	7.60	6.90	6.80	6.30	6.50	6.60	7.40	8.30	7.30	7.10	7.10
Professional services	7.75	7.92	7.08	7.67	6.50	6.83	7.58	7.17	7.75	7.50	7.83	7.33	7.08
Retail	7.25	7.00	6.63	7.38	6.50	6.00	7.25	6.88	7.38	6.63	7.88	6.50	6.50
Telecommunications	6.17	6.00	6.67	6.83	6.67	5.33	6.33	5.17	6.50	6.33	6.33	6.33	6.17
Travel and leisure	7.80	8.50	7.80	7.60	6.20	7.40	7.20	6.80	8.00	7.30	7.30	6.60	7.40
Average	7.43	7.35	7.35	7.48	6.53	6.83	7.09	6.75	7.46	7.43	7.42	7.09	7.15

TABLE 4 Survey average data plotted against the average for the retail industry

The retail industry is currently enjoying an upturn in sales which began in spring 2006 and has continued into the summer. This may very well have had a part to play in the strong showing of *Output, performance, quality and accountability* (J). It is also interesting, given this upsurge, that indicators L (*Empowerment*) and D (*Cooperation, support, interpersonal communication and relationships*) perform well.

It might be the case that, when the economy is buoyant and sales are on the up, team members really do feel more ready to take on more responsibility and, as a consequence, perceive themselves and the team as being more empowered. Equally, when there is an upward movement in sales, the team does have to work together and relationships improve to meet the challenge.

In contrast with relationships inside the team, those with other teams seem to fare less well (*Sound inter-group relations and communications*, F) as does dealing with change (*Change, creativity and challenging the status quo*, M). As sales and activity increase, maybe we should not be too surprised that team members are working hard to cope with the increased volume of activity and demand and are less likely to be taking the time and trouble to challenge the way things are done and search for improvements. The extra pressure may also reveal problems in the supply chain which might then colour the view people have of other parts of the business.

Perhaps we should not attempt to read too much into these results as far as the general economic climate is concerned. This is, after all, a sector that is affected very quickly by such changes, and it seems likely that we need to look for other, more relevant reasons behind the results.

Education

The scores for the education industry (Table 5 and Figure 9) are on average slightly higher than the survey average scores—particularly indicators C (*Openness, trust, confrontation and conflict resolution*), G (*Appropriate management/leadership*) and M (*Change, creativity and challenging the status quo*).

This seems to indicate that situations where team members are open with, and trust, one another are relatively frequent. The data also points to the possibility that, compared to other sectors, they seem more happy to confront issues that may arise between them, sharing information and feelings openly. This could be a consequence of a style of interaction in the sector which encourages the expression of different viewpoints. As a result, conflicts and disagreements that do arise seem to be resolved more successfully (indicator C: *Openness, trust, confrontation and conflict resolution*).

It seems that the style of leadership and management displayed within the teams is likely to be contributing positively towards how motivated and empowered the team members are feeling. There is a good balance between the amount of support and direction provided. Communication and feedback between management, individuals and the team as a whole are appropriate in terms of both quality and quantity (indicator G: *Appropriate management/leadership*). There could be many reasons for the higher score. It could be that the regular monitoring of schools' performance by Ofsted and the pressure of league tables has helped to engender a greater degree of accountability. Additionally, it may be the case that managers in this sector are often closer to their staff in ways of thinking since they have frequently 'done the job' themselves and may even still do it at times.

The scores the indicator on change and continuous improvement (M) are also relatively higher than other sec-

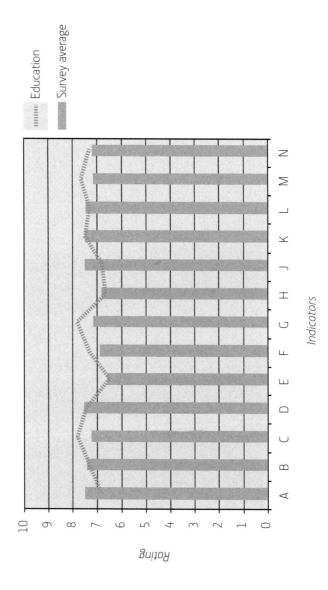

FIGURE 9 Survey average data plotted against the average for the education sector

	A	B	C	D	E	F	G	H	J	K	L	M	N
Education	6.83	7.33	7.83	7.50	6.50	7.33	7.83	6.67	6.83	7.50	7.33	7.67	7.33
Electronics and technology	7.43	7.14	7.71	8.29	6.57	7.57	6.86	7.29	6.86	7.86	7.43	7.14	7.71
Finance and insurance	8.50	7.25	7.75	7.50	6.25	7.25	7.25	7.50	7.75	7.50	8.25	7.50	7.50
Healthcare	6.20	5.80	6.60	6.20	6.20	6.80	6.40	5.80	7.60	6.20	6.40	5.60	6.80
Local government	7.40	6.90	7.60	6.90	6.80	6.30	6.50	6.60	7.40	8.30	7.30	7.10	7.10
Professional services	7.75	7.92	7.08	7.67	6.50	6.83	7.58	7.17	7.75	7.50	7.83	7.33	7.08
Retail	7.25	7.00	6.63	7.38	6.50	6.00	7.25	6.88	7.38	6.63	7.88	6.50	6.50
Telecommunications	6.17	6.00	6.67	6.83	6.67	5.33	6.33	5.17	6.50	6.33	6.33	6.33	6.17
Travel and leisure	7.80	8.50	7.80	7.60	6.20	7.40	7.20	6.80	8.00	7.30	7.30	6.60	7.40
Average	7.43	7.35	7.48	7.53	6.53	6.83	7.09	6.75	7.46	7.43	7.42	7.09	7.15

TABLE 5 Survey average data plotted against the average for the education sector

tors. It is possible that this is as a result of the many changes within the sector over the last two decades which have meant those remaining in, or entering, have become more used to change and working with it. Perhaps because they inhabit a learning environment, the teams are aware of, and use, a variety of 'creative thinking tools' and techniques in their discussions and meetings.

Interestingly, even for this sector, E (*Individual and team learning and development*) is the lowest-scoring indicator. It appears that working in the learning field does not preserve organisations from the general low score in this area.

Table 5 shows the second lowest-scoring indicator is H (*Sound team procedures and regular review*), at 6.67. As with the telecommunications industry, a score in this range would indicate that current team processes and procedures could benefit from a thorough review. Some, rather than helping, may actually be felt to be hindering the effectiveness of the team. It may be that some less value-adding processes can be eliminated or at least streamlined. Perhaps long-established processes have simply not been modified in response to changing circumstances. There could also be improvements in the way in which the team reviews its work.

Electronics and technology

In this industry sector *Cooperation, support, interpersonal communication and relationships* (D) is the highest-scoring indicator with a very high average of 8.29 (Table 6 and Figure 10).

Employees in this industry sector are often engineers and technical experts; in this kind of working environment (rather than an office environment), camaraderie and interpersonal bonds can be very strong because the focus is on task rather than person. It is possible that this could lead to good cooperation between team members and mutual trust based on the technical expertise that each possesses. This may well account for the relatively high score for this indicator.

This is mirrored in the similarly high score of 7.71 in indicator C (*Openness, trust, confrontation and conflict resolution*). This is the joint-third highest-scoring indicator (with indicator N [*Decision-making and problem-solving*]), and shows that team members are open with, and trust, one another. Consequently, they are happy to confront any issues that may arise between them, sharing information and feelings openly. Where conflicts and disagreements do arise, they are usually resolved successfully.

The lowest indicator for this industry is indicator E (*Individual and team learning and development*). As outlined in the previous chapter on aggregate analysis, indicator E seems to be a universal development area for almost 50% of the industries surveyed.

Not far behind are G and J, also areas that would benefit from some specific attention.

Appropriate management/leadership (G) could be an issue given the very nature of an industry that is made up largely of people, including managers, whose natural style is to focus more on the task than the person. They may therefore be less disposed to 'tune in' to team members' feelings and to adopt a highly directive approach at the expense of some of the more supporting (softer) behaviours. At times this may well have an impact on the motivation and empowerment within the team. Perhaps communication and feedback between management, individuals and the team as a whole is not as frequent in quality and quantity as it could be.

Output, performance, quality and accountability (J) indicates that there is a general feeling the quality of productivity could be improved and quantity may also be questionable. It may be

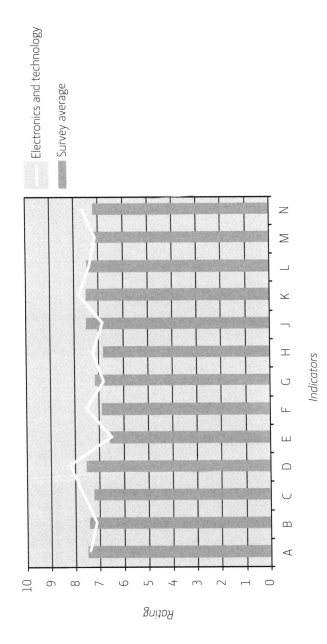

FIGURE 10   Survey average data plotted against the average for the electronics and technology industry

	A	B	C	D	E	F	G	H	J	K	L	M	N
Education	6.83	7.33	7.83	7.50	6.50	7.33	7.83	6.67	6.83	7.50	7.33	7.67	7.33
Electronics and technology	7.43	7.14	7.71	8.29	6.57	7.57	6.86	7.29	6.86	7.86	7.43	7.14	7.71
Finance and insurance	8.50	7.25	7.75	7.50	6.25	7.25	7.50	7.75	7.50	8.25	7.50	7.50	
Healthcare	6.20	5.80	6.60	6.20	6.20	6.80	6.40	5.80	7.60	6.20	6.40	5.60	6.80
Local government	7.40	6.90	7.60	6.90	6.80	6.30	6.50	6.60	7.40	8.30	7.30	7.10	7.10
Professional services	7.75	7.92	7.08	7.67	6.50	6.83	7.58	7.17	7.75	7.50	7.83	7.33	7.08
Retail	7.25	7.00	6.63	7.38	6.50	6.00	7.25	6.88	7.38	6.63	7.88	6.50	6.50
Telecommunications	6.17	6.00	6.67	6.83	6.67	5.33	6.33	5.17	6.50	6.33	6.33	6.33	6.17
Travel and leisure	7.80	8.50	7.80	7.60	6.20	7.40	7.20	6.80	8.00	7.30	7.30	6.60	7.40
Average	7.43	7.35	7.48		6.53	6.83	7.09	6.75	7.46	7.43	7.42	7.09	7.15

TABLE 6 Survey average data plotted against the average for the electronics and technology industry

that this is a perception created by the very type of team member and the high emphasis the team member is likely to place on things being done to high standards.

Finance and insurance

The range between the highest-scoring and lowest-scoring indicator is very large for the finance and insurance industry results (Table 7 and Figure 11). It peaks at a high of 8.50 for indicator A (*Balanced roles*) and then drops to a low of 6.25 for indicator E (*Individual and team learning and development*).

This industry sector is possibly the one in which there are the greatest number of constantly moving variables. Changes in legislation; takeovers and mergers; the ease and frequency with which new products and services are introduced; new players entering the market; and the fierce competition both nationally and internationally all provide significant challenges. Employees expectations are possibly higher because of the continuous need to learn about new products and services, but pressure to hit challenging targets can be extremely intense and therefore does not allow much time for learning.

The low score on G (*Appropriate management/leadership*) is perhaps a result of all the changes and pressures; because of some quite rapid growth, the average age of managers and team leaders has been reducing, possibly with a corresponding decrease in leadership behaviour and skill levels.

The relatively higher scores in A (*Balanced roles*) and L (*Empowerment*) are possibly the result of fairly clear lines of demarcation over who should do what (e.g. a traditional split between sales and administration) and, as a response to the many changes, there being plenty of opportunities for employees and team members to take initiatives and feel responsible for their own decisions and actions. The latter is a counterpoint to the lack of leadership direction in certain quarters. It could also be a manifestation of the sales nature of this industry where success is often rewarded, and substantially at that, on an individual basis.

Healthcare

Included in this category are organisations as diverse as pharmaceutical companies and health trusts. Given this, establishing any significant trends could have been problematic. However, the majority were from the NHS (National Health Service) area and the results that emerged seem to have a degree of consistency with what could be expected from a sector that has been under considerable public and political scrutiny and has experienced a lot of painful cuts, closures and job losses. These results indicate that the healthcare profession scores much lower than the average in most of the indicators, in a similar way to the telecommunications industry (Table 8 and Figure 12).

The highest indicators are J (*Output, performance, quality and accountability*), F (*Sound inter-group relations and communications*) and N (*Decision-making and problem-solving*) and this fits the picture of an environment where patient care and sometimes life and death issues hang on the nature of decisions made and teams are likely to have well-established decision-making procedures and practices in place. The various teams within such organisations also liaise well towards the common purpose of patient care provision and the overall result is that there is a

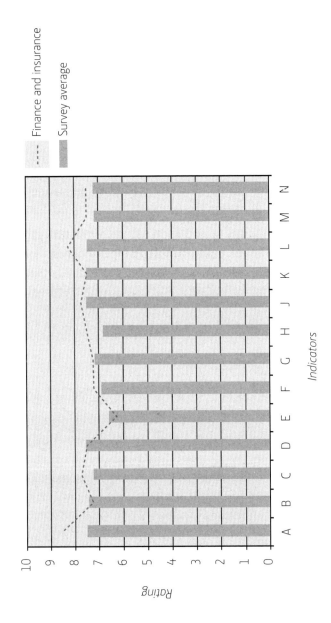

FIGURE 11 Survey average data plotted against the average for the finance and insurance industry

	A	B	C	D	E	F	G	H	J	K	L	M	N
Education	6.83	7.33	7.83	7.50	6.50	7.33	7.83	6.67	6.83	7.50	7.33	7.67	7.33
Electronics and technology	7.43	7.14	7.71	8.29	6.57	7.57	6.86	7.29	6.86	7.86	7.43	7.14	7.71
Finance and insurance	8.50	7.25	7.75	7.50	6.25	7.25	7.25	7.50	7.75	7.50	8.25	7.50	7.50
Healthcare	6.20	5.80	6.60	6.20	6.20	6.80	6.40	5.80	7.60	6.20	6.40	5.60	6.80
Local government	7.40	6.90	7.60	6.90	6.80	6.30	6.50	6.60	7.40	8.30	7.30	7.10	7.10
Professional services	7.75	7.92	7.08	7.67	6.50	6.83	7.58	7.17	7.75	7.50	7.83	7.33	7.08
Retail	7.25	7.00	6.63	7.38	6.50	6.00	7.25	6.88	7.38	6.63	7.88	6.50	6.50
Telecommunications	6.17	6.00	6.67	6.83	6.67	5.33	6.33	5.17	6.50	6.33	6.33	6.33	6.17
Travel and leisure	7.80	8.50	7.80	7.60	6.20	7.40	7.20	6.80	8.00	7.30	7.30	6.60	7.40
Average	7.43	7.35	7.48	7.53	6.53	6.83	7.09	6.75	7.46	7.43	7.42	7.09	7.15

TABLE 7 Survey average data plotted against the average for the finance and insurance industry

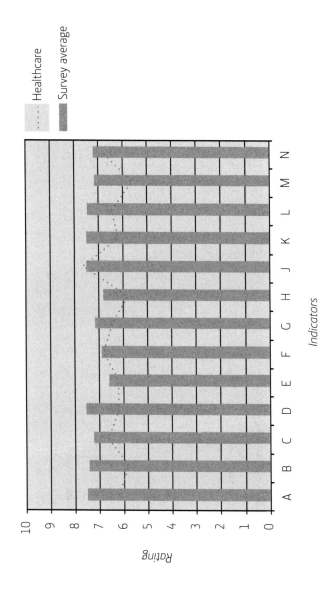

FIGURE 12 Survey average data plotted against the average for the healthcare sector

	A	B	C	D	E	F	G	H	J	K	L	M	N
Education	6.83	7.33	7.83	7.50	6.50	7.33	7.83	6.67	6.83	7.50	7.33	7.67	7.33
Electronics and technology	7.43	7.14	7.71	8.29	6.57	7.57	6.86	7.29	6.86	7.86	7.43	7.14	7.71
Finance and insurance	8.50	7.25	7.75	7.50	6.25	7.25	7.25	7.50	7.75	7.50	8.25	7.50	7.50
Healthcare	6.20	5.80	6.60	6.20	6.20	6.80	6.40	5.80	7.60	6.20	6.40	5.60	6.80
Local government	7.40	6.90	7.60	6.90	6.80	6.30	6.50	6.60	7.40	8.30	7.30	7.10	7.10
Professional services	7.75	7.92	7.08	7.67	6.50	6.83	7.58	7.17	7.75	7.50	7.83	7.33	7.08
Retail	7.25	7.00	6.63	7.38	6.50	6.00	7.25	6.88	7.38	6.63	7.88	6.50	6.50
Telecommunications	6.17	6.00	6.67	6.83	6.67	5.33	6.33	5.17	6.50	6.33	6.33	6.33	6.17
Travel and leisure	7.80	8.50	7.80	7.60	6.20	7.40	7.20	6.80	8.00	7.30	7.30	6.60	7.40
Average	7.43	7.35	7.35	7.48	6.53	6.83	7.09	6.75	7.46	7.43	7.42	7.09	7.15

TABLE 8 Survey average data plotted against the average for the healthcare sector

sense of achievement and real meaning to their work and the results they get.

What is surprising among the lower indicator scores is the presence of *Clear objectives and purpose* (B), and it clearly would require a more detailed survey and analysis to understand what is behind such a relatively low score. The appearance of *Change, creativity and challenging the status quo* (M) is a little more readily explained. With so many changes being imposed from outside and with acute pressure on numbers, resources, etc., it becomes difficult for teams to find the time and will to act in a way which, at least in the short term, may involve significant upheavals.

Local government

The range of scores in this sector is exactly 2 (a low of 6.3 to a high of 8.3), which places it in the middle of the spread of scoring ranges recorded among the sectors we examined (the lowest range is 1.66 and the highest 2.33). However, the actual scoring still provides indications of how teams are operating (Table 9 and Figure 13). There is less of a swing in perceived team operations compared to the other public sector in the survey (education, with a 2.33 range between the highest and lowest scores).

In an area where there is a public perception of strong union activity, at least among manual employees, and a more 'caring' culture, it is interesting to find that F (*Sound inter-group relations and communications*), G (*Appropriate management/leadership*) and H (*Sound team procedures and regular review*) come out lowest. Although things are now changing and managers are more frequently moving between the private and public sectors, there seems to remain a view that team leadership could be more effective. This may be related to a historic tendency to be reluctant to tackle performance issues and to reward good performers adequately. It may also contribute to the feeling that team procedures are not really reviewed and certain practices continue with little, if any, effort to amend or replace them.

The results indicate that people are clear on what their role and function within the team is (A: *Balanced roles*)—perhaps not too surprising given the slow rate of change that has often typified local government. Things also look good with indicator C (*Openness, trust, confrontation and conflict resolution*), which raises the question: is this because conflicts are well handled or is it because they are avoided owing to the prevailing culture?

Professional services

This sector recorded one of the highest scores out of the survey as a whole (Table 10 and Figure 14). Owing to the size of organisations in this sector, often not large by national standards, and the nature of their client relationships, the commercial imperative means that everyone appreciates how important they are both individually and as a team for the continued success of the organisation.

Certainly, there is some evidence to support this view in the outcomes, with the strongest indicators falling in the areas of roles, objectives and empowerment (B [*Clear objectives and purpose*], A [*Balanced roles*] and L [*Empowerment*]). Team members not only feel clear about what their team has to achieve and what everyone's role is but also are flexible and see themselves as

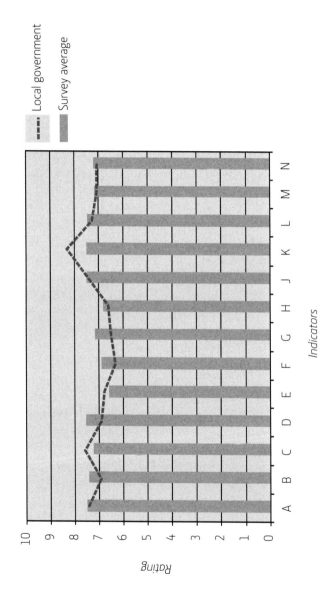

FIGURE 13 Survey average data plotted against the average for the local government sector

	A	B	C	D	E	F	G	H	J	K	L	M	N
Education	6.83	7.33	7.83	7.50	6.50	7.33	7.83	6.67	6.83	7.50	7.33	7.67	7.33
Electronics and technology	7.43	7.14	7.71	8.29	6.57	7.57	6.86	7.29	6.86	7.86	7.43	7.14	7.71
Finance and insurance	8.50	7.25	7.75	7.50	6.25	7.25	7.25	7.50	7.75	7.50	8.25	7.50	7.50
Healthcare	6.20	5.80	6.60	6.20	6.20	6.80	6.40	5.80	7.60	6.20	6.40	5.60	6.80
Local government	7.40	6.90	7.60	6.90	6.80	6.30	6.50	6.60	7.40	8.30	7.30	7.10	7.10
Professional services	7.75	7.92	7.08	7.67	6.50	6.83	7.58	7.17	7.75	7.50	7.83	7.33	7.08
Retail	7.25	7.00	6.63	7.38	6.50	6.00	7.25	6.88	7.38	6.63	7.88	6.50	6.50
Telecommunications	6.17	6.00	6.67	6.83	6.67	5.33	6.33	5.17	6.50	6.33	6.33	6.33	6.17
Travel and leisure	7.80	8.50	7.80	7.60	6.20	7.40	7.20	6.80	8.00	7.30	7.30	6.60	7.40
Average	7.43	7.35	7.48	6.53	6.83	7.09	6.75	7.46	7.43	7.42	7.09	7.15	

TABLE 9 Survey average data plotted against the average for the local government sector

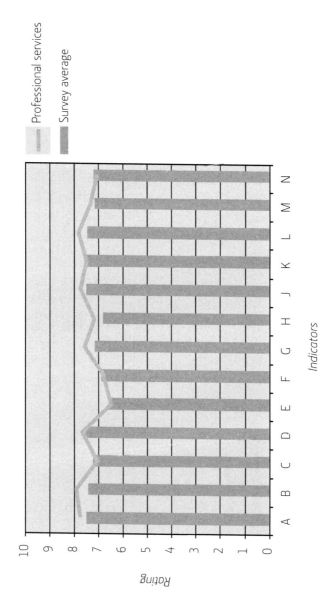

FIGURE 14 Survey average data plotted against the average for the professional services sector

	A	B	C	D	E	F	G	H	J	K	L	M	N
Education	6.83	7.33	7.83	7.50	6.50	7.33	7.83	6.67	6.83	7.50	7.33	7.67	7.33
Electronics and technology	7.43	7.14	7.71	8.29	6.57	7.57	6.86	7.29	6.86	7.86	7.43	7.14	7.71
Finance and insurance	8.50	7.25	7.75	7.50	6.25	7.25	7.25	7.50	7.75	7.50	8.25	7.50	7.50
Healthcare	6.20	5.80	6.60	6.20	6.20	6.80	6.40	5.80	7.60	6.20	6.40	5.60	6.80
Local government	7.40	6.90	7.60	6.90	6.80	6.30	6.50	6.60	7.40	8.30	7.30	7.10	7.10
Professional services	7.75	7.92	7.08	7.67	6.50	6.83	7.58	7.17	7.75	7.50	7.83	7.33	7.08
Retail	7.25	7.00	6.63	7.38	6.50	6.00	7.25	6.88	7.38	6.63	7.88	6.50	6.50
Telecommunications	6.17	6.00	6.67	6.83	6.67	5.33	6.33	5.17	6.50	6.33	6.33	6.33	6.17
Travel and leisure	7.80	8.50	7.80	7.60	6.20	7.40	7.20	6.80	8.00	7.30	7.30	6.60	7.40
Average	7.43	7.35	7.35	7.48	6.53	6.83	7.09	6.75	7.46	7.43	7.42	7.09	7.15

TABLE 10 Survey average data plotted against the average for the professional services sector

being authorised to make proposals and take decisions that they believe to be appropriate.

Lower scores in E (*Individual and team learning and development*), F (*Sound inter-group relations and communications*) and L (*Empowerment*) also seem consistent. Learning and development is a somewhat unexpected shortcoming given the general trend for all industries in the survey. The poor scoring on relations between groups seems to be partly explained by the fact that often in professional services teams work very closely with an outside client without there being any particularly strong need for them to be liaising closely with other teams in their own organisation. As a consequence, the score for this indicator may not be too much of a cause for concern though nonetheless meriting some exploration; the same applies to indicator C (*Openness, trust, confrontation and conflict resolution*).

Travel and leisure

Of all the industry sectors we included, this is probably the most competitive (Table 11 and Figure 15). Factors such as: competition from low-cost airlines; changes to the way people take holidays (from package to arranging own; two-week breaks to small mini-breaks); the emergence of the internet; and a whole range of others have created pressures on margins that mean going out of business is even more of a likelihood for a travel/leisure company than for many others.

Yet, despite all of this and perhaps even because of it, the results hold up very favourably against the survey average. Could it be that the 'Manchester United effect' of pulling together as a team to meet the external challenges is playing a part here?

Certainly the strengths (B [*Clear objectives and purpose*], J [*Output, performance, quality and accountability*] and A [*Balanced roles*]) that emerge parallel those in the above analogy. Aims and objectives (B) score well so people are clear on exactly what needs to be achieved and who plays which part. Output and performance quality (J) are good and receive attention: generally, this is an industry that actively seeks feedback from its customers and heeds the responses it gets—all of which will contribute to the above-survey-average scores for these indicators.

The downside is that the pressure on the industry seems to be resulting in a poor showing for *Individual and team learning and development* (E)—not out of line with the general findings for all the sectors but below the average. More interestingly, and not a little worrying, is the fact that indicator M (*Change, creativity and challenging the status quo*) is also one of the poorest for teams in this sector. At a time when the status quo in the industry is being shaken by some of the factors referred to above, there is a need for teams to become more challenging of accepted ways and to find additional creativity and innovation.

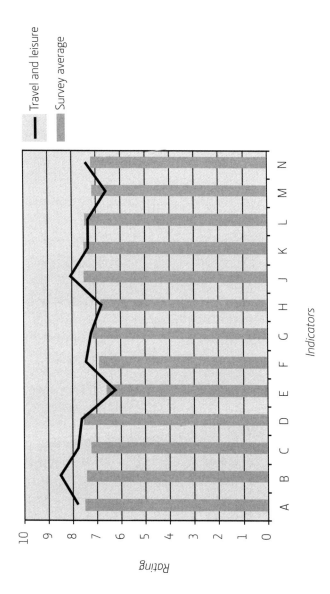

FIGURE 15 Survey average data plotted against the average for the travel and leisure industry

	A	B	C	D	E	F	G	H	J	K	L	M	N
Education	6.83	7.33	7.83	7.50	6.50	7.33	7.83	6.67	6.83	7.50	7.33	7.67	7.33
Electronics and technology	7.43	7.14	7.71	8.29	6.57	7.57	6.86	7.29	6.86	7.86	7.43	7.14	7.71
Finance and insurance	8.50	7.25	7.75	7.50	6.25	7.25	7.25	7.50	7.75	7.50	8.25	7.50	7.50
Healthcare	6.20	5.80	6.60	6.20	6.20	6.80	6.40	5.80	7.60	6.20	6.40	5.60	6.80
Local government	7.40	6.90	7.60	6.90	6.80	6.30	6.50	6.60	7.40	8.30	7.30	7.10	7.10
Professional services	7.75	7.92	7.08	7.67	6.50	6.83	7.58	7.17	7.75	7.50	7.83	7.33	7.08
Retail	7.25	7.00	6.63	7.38	6.50	6.00	7.25	6.88	7.38	6.63	7.88	6.50	6.50
Telecommunications	6.17	6.00	6.67	6.83	6.67	5.33	6.33	5.17	6.50	6.33	6.33	6.33	6.17
Travel and leisure	7.80	8.50	7.80	7.60	6.20	7.40	7.20	6.80	8.00	7.30	7.30	6.60	7.40
Average	7.43	7.35	7.48	7.35	6.53	6.83	7.09	6.75	7.46	7.43	7.42	7.09	7.15

TABLE 11 Survey average data plotted against the average for the travel and leisure industry

5

The roadmap to team effectiveness

Introduction

Throughout this research we have been trying to make links between the nature of the industry, the sort of people that work in it and current trends in the sector in order to make sense of and interpret the results. Of course, it is not as simple as that.

In many ways, our results pose more questions than they may answer. This is really for two reasons. The first is the wide spread of teams involved. The second is the relatively simple level at which the survey has been carried out. Only one question was asked with regard to each indicator. In the full Team Performance Diagnostic (TPD) there would be 12 questions asked about each of the 13 indicators. This would make it possible to drill into the answers and identify the specific areas where the team was doing well and those where attention was required and exactly what the solutions might be.

While we have suggested some reasons in various industry sectors for certain scores, these can at best be educated guesses. Without the detailed examination that a full TPD would afford, it is impossible to validate the reasons and, more importantly, start to take the necessary actions to improve the performance, effectiveness and efficiency of the team in question.

Team size and Key Performance Indicators

One thing we were keen to discover from the study was what differences, if any, team size played in the success of a particular indicator.

As the previous chapters show, some distinct differences emerged. Looking first at the average results of all indicators for the teams' sizes, it is interesting that small teams (10 or fewer) emerge best at 7.39 followed by large teams (20 plus) at 7.12, and medium-sized (10–20) lowest at 6.95. This appears to show that the smallest teams are the best performing over all areas. This could be owing to the easier communications and more manageable numbers leading to fewer conflicts, less misunderstanding, clearer sight of and appreciation of what others are doing and how they are contributing to the team effort. Large teams possibly score more highly than middle-sized because as the team grows beyond a certain size there is a more pressing necessity for things to be coordinated and organised, otherwise chaos will obviously ensue. As a consequence, the large teams address this issue while the medium-sized ones are less likely to see the need to do anything about it.

It is especially interesting to examine the indicators where the average trend plotted according to team size seems to digress from the general, aggregate result (see Figure 16 and Table 12).

Large teams record lower results than middle-sized for *Empowerment* (L), *Change, creativity and challenging the status quo* (M), *Decision-making and problem-solving* (N) and *Sound inter-group relations and communications* (F). They post higher results than small teams for *Individual and team learning and development* (E), *Appropriate management/leadership* (G), *Sound team procedures and regular review* (H) and *Output, performance, quality and accountability* (J). However, all of these would seem entirely consistent with the logic of the argument already expressed.

Considering the lowest and highest scores, the different-sized teams' records also allows us to suggest some interesting ideas.

The smaller teams do best with D (*Cooperation, support, interpersonal communication and relationships*), C (*Openness, trust, confrontation and conflict resolution*) and K (*Morale*). Therefore it appears reasonable to conclude that the fewer the numbers the easier it is for trust to be built up and for people to know and understand each other a little better, so as to be able to cooperate well together and to share views, opinions and information readily. Behaving in this way will, unsurprisingly, have a positive impact on morale.

The weakest indicators for smaller teams, E (*Individual and team learning and development*) and H (*Sound team procedures and regular review*), again appear to fit a rough sort of logic. With small teams, the requirement to both implement and regularly review team process and procedure will be less obvious and pressing. Equally, with fewer internal team resources to call on, it is highly likely that less time will be devoted to devel-

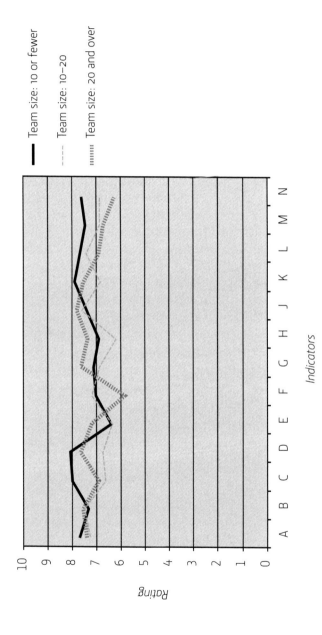

FIGURE 16 **Ratings by team size**

	A	B	C	D	E	F	G	H	J	K	L	M	N
0–10	7.63	7.33	7.90	7.98	6.44	7.02	7.09	6.91	7.40	7.81	7.63	7.42	7.56
10–20	7.25	7.46	6.67	6.75	6.42	7.17	6.88	6.25	7.54	6.83	7.38	6.88	6.88
20+	7.33	7.50	6.92	7.58	7.17	5.92	7.58	7.33	7.75	7.50	6.92	6.75	6.33

TABLE 12 Ratings by team size

oping team members. (This also seems to hold true for middle-sized teams but not for the larger ones where the greater numbers possibly allow people to be released to train and develop.)

Interestingly, the medium-sized teams do best on J (*Output, performance, quality and accountability*) and B (*Clear objectives and purpose*), reinforcing the direct link between clear objectives and purpose and productive output. By paying less attention to the softer issues, where small teams seem to have an almost natural advantage, and spending less effort on procedural issues, unlike bigger teams, they are perhaps better able to concentrate on target areas. While good in the short term, over time this imbalance may become counterproductive as relations could become strained and more conflicts emerge. Indeed, it is in just these indicators (H [*Sound team procedures and regular review*] and C [*Openness, trust, confrontation and conflict resolution*]) that these teams fare least well. Failure to attend to learning and development (E) is also likely to create longer-term difficulties.

Looking at teams of size 20 and above, there is a very noticeable low point at indicator F (*Sound inter-group relations and communications*). This suggests that the size of the team has a direct impact on the way in which it interacts with other teams in the organisation. This indicates that within the teams of larger size relationships and communication channels between this team and other areas of the business may be weak. Individuals and teams from other departments may not regard the team entirely positively, or have mixed views. The team may feel isolated from other parts of the organisation, not knowing what some other people do, or even who they are. There may be a lack of effective cross-team working relationships and communications. Possibly the team has reached such a size that there is a tendency to see itself as completely independent of the rest of the organisation and so putting less effort into creating and maintaining some of the cross-functional relationships that can prove so valuable.

Managing change

Managers often focus on the structural and systemic aspects of an organisation while ignoring the underlying irrational and covert dynamics that impact interpersonal relations. The results are often low workplace morale, declining productivity and high costs of recruitment, development and retention.

Human performance improvement and organisational effectiveness are the ultimate responsibility of organisational leaders. Teamwork cohesiveness appeared strongly related with team members' attitudes towards the organisation. Cohesiveness between team members was positively associated with core value and negatively with merit and performance. In addition, skills appeared strongly related to team satisfaction.

Business success today mandates the use of these high-performance work teams throughout our organisations.

Employees' resistance involves all the mechanisms that protect them from an experience that they view as dangerous. Anxiety and resistance among any organisation's employees will not quickly disappear and it will take time and effort to work through and overcome it. Insight is not easily obtained and the success of any organisational intervention depends on managers' abilities to overcome employee resistance (Kanter 1983).

Participative management has nowadays become the accepted route for institutions to take to allow employees to participate with management in making decisions that effect the organisation and their work roles in it—as well as to improve their performance (Olsen and Eadie 1982).

The principles of re-engineering necessarily require not only a sea change in the way people work, but also a radical new approach to management (Champy 1995). Most organisational structures in the various sectors are in urgent need of a strategy to re-engineer their management; it can be achieved with the same management personnel, but it is unlikely to succeed where the corporate atmosphere is charged with fear.

It was so much simpler in the past. Organisations hired people to work *for* them. So they selected them, appraised them, and rewarded them for their ability to perform a specific task. But that approach is no longer relevant. Today's business climate demands that we hire people to work *with* us, as part of a community of shared aspirations, ideas and trust.

Today, effectively managed organisations will have restructured their organisational charts. In particular, organisations need to become more decentralised, moving decision-making power into the hands of those individuals doing the job.

Carnall (2003) argues that, where fundamental change is required, we must first look at how managers see the problems. First and foremost, we need to review managerial performance.

Finally, it is important to note that many of the organisations examined are finding that the TPD has helped them to: *improve results and reach higher levels of team performance; and quickly establish how to generate fast improvements in team effectiveness and undertake development activities that maximise team performance.*

Key conclusions and recommendations

An organisation's most important asset is its people (Dixon 1991). People are the wealth-creators, and therefore all managers need to develop employees' potential by using their skills and imagination to help their institutions to grow and also to determine their roles in the wider environment.

The study supports the view that people must learn how to communicate effectively in teams and between teams across the entire organisation. Employees must use communication to resolve and manage conflicts, and to air and resolve grievances and complaints.

Working in teams requires that managers learn to adopt a supportive style in their relations with others; they need to learn patience, and an ability to stand back and let the groups reach their own decisions (Drucker 1998). Team leaders and upper management need to learn how to act as role models for team behaviour, and how to promote the active building, leadership and management of teams. They should look to create a direct link between all departments and with senior management, to improve the systematic communication and quality of information. The quality of relationships between divisions and departments also needs to be promoted and nurtured, as most institutions will suffer from inter-departmental conflicts.

Managers and directors have to consider how their organisations' priorities will adapt to changing conditions. They must realise that no meaningful, lasting change is possible without a certain amount of insight into why resistance to change occurs; and a systematic effort is required to dismantle the most dysfunctional aspects of this resistance.

Managing projects, setting goals, clarifying roles and solving problems in teams are all skills that must be developed.

These new organisational skills are essential if teams are to operate effectively and efficiently.

Any organisation's management should definitely consider *front-to-back responsibility* for the organisation's core activities, negotiating overall performance targets with staff, and sharing skills, knowledge, experience and problems with them.

Employees need help in overcoming fears about the loss of job security and independence, and to learn how to continue to make individual contributions within team structures.

The study indicates that interpersonal skills need to be developed within the various UK sectors:

- Better social awareness, social decision-making, conflict-resolution skills, understanding others, self-control and planning for solving cognitive tasks

- More thinking before acting, helpful, considerate, concerned, pro-social strategies for interpersonal problem-solving, skill in handling interpersonal problems, willingness to cooperate and empathy

- Improved communication skills, problem-solving skills, interpersonal effectiveness and improvement in emotion, recognition and understanding

Finally, the research suggests that the use of the TPD tool contributes to more free-flowing feedback within and between teams. Its use enables organisational leaders to continually sharpen their awareness of what is going on in their teams. This also encourages them to focus on the development of their own leadership skills which in turn helps to promote an organisational climate that fosters effective teamwork. Such a positive organisational culture is a major contributor to success in all organisations, irrespective of the sector. It also leads to the growth of human capital, which will lead to higher team performance. As a result, many organisations that are world-class at managing materials and machinery will become as effective in managing the human side of their activities as well.

Bibliography

Amabile, M. (1998) 'How to kill creativity', *Harvard Business Review*, September–October 1998: 77-87.

Arthur, B., and L. Aiman-Smith (2001) 'Gain sharing and organizational learning', *Academy of Management Journal* 44: 737-55.

Avolio, J. (1999) *Full Leadership Development: Building the Vital Forces in Organizations* (Thousand Oaks, CA: Sage Publications): 15.

Baron, R.A., and D. Byrne (1991) *Social Psychology: Understanding Human Interaction* (Boston, MA: Allyn & Bacon, 6th edn).

——, D. Byrne and N.R. Branscombe (2007) *Mastering Social Psychology* (Boston, MA: Pearson/Allyn & Bacon).

Beer, M., B. Spector, P. Lawrence, D. Quinn Mills and R. Walton (1984) *Managing Human Assets* (New York: The Free Press): 1.

Besser, L. (1995) 'Rewards and organizational goals achievement', *Journal of Management Studies* 32: 383-401.

Bozeman, B., and J.D. Straussman (1990) *Public Management Strategies* (San Francisco: Jossey-Bass Publishers).

Bryant, A., and G. Harvey (2000) *Acute Stress Disorder* (Washington, DC: American Psychological Association).

Carnall, C.A. (2003) *Managing Change in Organizations* (FT/Pearson Education, 4th edn).

Carrie, L. (1985) 'The effects of group cohesiveness and leader behavior on decision processes', *Journal of Management* 11.1: 5-18.

Champy, J. (1995) *Reengineering Management: The Mandate for New Leadership* (New York: HarperBusiness).

Clampitt, G., R. DeKock and T. Cashman (2000) 'A strategy for communicating about uncertainty', *Academy of Management Executive* 14.4: 41-57.

Costa, C., A. Roe and T. Taillieu (2001) 'Trust within teams: the relation with performance effectiveness', *European Journal of Work and Organizational Psychology* 10.3: 302-30.

Dixon, R. (1991) *Management Theory and Practice* (Oxford: Butterworth-Heinemann).

Drucker, P. (1998) 'The coming of the new organization', *Harvard Business Review*, January–February 1998: 45-53.

Galagan, A. (1994) 'Reinventing the profession', *Training and Development* 48.12 (December 1994): 20-27.

Ghoshal, S., J. Lampel, H. Mintzberg and J.B. Quinn (2003) *The Strategy Process* (London: FT Prentice Hall, 4th edn).

Greg, L., M. Charles and S. Henry (1999) *Teamwork and Group Dynamics* (New York: John Wiley): 139-41.

Haberberg, A., and A. Reiple (2001) *The Strategic Management of Organisations* (London: FT Prentice Hall).

Hersey, P., H. Blanchard and E. Johnson (2001) *Leading Management of Organizational Behavior: Human Resources* (Englewood Cliffs, NJ: Prentice Hall, 8th edn).

Hofstede, G. (1991) *Cultures and Organizations: Software of the Mind* (London: McGraw-Hill).

Huczynski, A., and D. Buchanan (2006) *Organizational Behaviour: An Introductory* (London: Prentice Hall, 6th edn).

Hughes, O.E. (1998) *Public Management and Administration: An Introduction* (London: Macmillan).

Johnson, G., K. Scholes and R. Whittington (2005) *Exploring Corporate Strategy: Text and Cases* (London: FT Prentice Hall).

Joyce, P. (1999) *Strategic Management for the Public Services* (Buckingham, UK: Open University Press).

Kanter, R.M. (1983) *The Change Masters* (New York: Simon & Schuster).

Katzenbach, J., and S. Douglas (1993) 'The discipline of teams', *Harvard Business Review*, March–April 1993: 111-20.

Kraft, R. (1999) *Utilizing Self-managing Teams: Effective Behavior of Team Leaders* (Hamden, CN: Garland).

Kramer, M. (1999) 'Trust and distrust in organizations: emerging perspectives, enduring questions', *Annual Review of Psychology* 50: 580-89.

LaFasto, F., and E. Larson (2001) *When Teams Work Best* (Thousand Oaks, CA: Sage Publications).

Latham, P. (2001) 'The importance of understanding and changing employee outcome expectancies for gaining commitment to an organizational goal', *Personnel Psychology* 54: 707-16.

Legge, K. (1989) 'Human resource management: a critical analysis', in J. Storey (ed.), *New Perspectives on Human Resource Management* (London: Routledge).

Luhmann, N. (1979) *Trust and Power* (New York: John Wiley).

Lynch, R. (2003) *Corporate Strategy* (London: FT Prentice Hall, 3rd edn).

Maslow, A. (1970) *Motivation and Personality* (New York: Harper & Row, 2nd edn).

McLagan, P.A. (1989) 'Models for HRD practice', *Training and Development Journal* 43.9: 49-59.

Meyerson, D.E. (2001) 'Radical change: the quiet way', *Harvard Business Review* 79.9: 92-104.

Michalski, W., and D. King (1998) *Forty Tools for Cross-functional Teams* (Portland, OR: Productivity Press).

Needle, D. (2001) *Business in Context: An Introduction to Business and its Environment* (London: Thomson Learning, 3rd edn).

Nelson, M. (1995) 'Interpersonal team leadership skills', *Hospital Material Management Quarterly* 16.4: 53-63.

Olsen, J.B., and D.C. Eadie (1982) *The Game Plan: Governance with Foresight* (Washington, DC: Council on State Planning Agencies).

Osborn, D., and L. Moran (2000) *The New Self-directed Work Teams* (Blacklick, OH: McGraw-Hill, 2nd edn).

Pettinger, R. (2001) *Mastering Management Skills* (Palgrave Master Series; London: Palgrave Macmillan).

Rousseau, M. (2001) 'The idiosyncratic deal: flexibility versus fairness', *Organizational Dynamics* 29.4: 260-73.

Saunders, M., P. Lewis and A. Thornhill (2007) *Research Methods for Business Students* (London: Prentice Hall, 3rd edn).

Smith, F. (1999) 'Difficulty, consequences and effort in academic task performance', *Psychological Report* 85: 869-80.

Stewart, A. (1993) 'Reengineering: the hot new managing tool', *Fortune*, 23 August 1993: 41-48.

Tepper, J., D. Lockhart and J. Hoobler (2001) 'Justice, citizenship and role definition effects', *Journal of Applied Psychology* 86.4: 789-96.

Thamhain, H.J., and D.L. Wilemon (1975) 'Conflict management in project life cycles', *Sloan Management Review* 17: 31-50.

VandeWalle, D., W.L. Corn and J.W. Slocum (2001) 'The role of goal orientation following performance feedback', *Journal of Applied Psychology* 86: 629-40.

White, A. (1994) 'Developing leaders for the high-performance workplace', *Human Resource Management* 33.1 (Spring 1994): 161-65.

William, F. (1999) 'Anonymity and other keys to successful problem-solving meetings', *National Productivity Review* 8 (Spring 1999): 145-56.

Yarbrough, T. (2002) *Leading Groups and Teams* (Mason, OH: Thomson Learning).

Zhou, J., and M. George (2001) 'When job dissatisfaction leads to creativity', *Academy of Management Journal* 44: 682-96.

The 13 Key Performance Indicators

A Balanced roles
B Clear objectives and purpose
C Openness, trust, confrontation and conflict resolution
D Cooperation, support, interpersonal communication and relationships
E Individual and team learning and development
F Sound inter-group relations and communications
G Appropriate management/leadership
H Sound team procedures and regular review
J Output, performance, quality and accountability
K Morale
L Empowerment
M Change, creativity and challenging the status quo
N Decision-making and problem-solving

The 13 Key Performance Indicators are described below with an indication of what 'good' looks like in a healthy team in respect of each one. If 'good' becomes the benchmark, then the team can analyse where they are against that benchmark, what causes it and what they can do about it. Empowerment stops being management-speak and becomes reality.

A: Balanced roles

People understand both their own and other team members' roles. There is flexibility within the team and a preparedness and ability to help each other. Work is allocated according to individuals' capabilities and skills. There is a good sense that we have the right expertise and that we are well balanced as a working team.

B: Clear objectives and purpose

The team has a well-communicated 'purpose', and objectives are clearly defined. Team members fully understand their own objectives and the way in which they can contribute towards achieving the team's goals. There is a good sense that team members are all 'pulling in the same direction'. There is a good balance between time spent on 'doing' and on necessary 'planning'.

C: Openness, trust, confrontation and conflict resolution

Team members are open with, and trust, one another. Consequently, they are happy to confront any issues that may arise between them, sharing information and feelings openly. Consequently, conflicts and disagreements that do arise are usually resolved successfully.

D: Cooperation, support, interpersonal communication and relationships

Team members cooperate with and support one another, helping each other out when the pressure is on. There is good interpersonal communication and relationships within the team are strong. Listening to one another is a key strength of this team, as is mutual trust between team members. Team members give each other appropriate and useful feedback aimed at improving individual and team performance.

E: Individual and team learning and development

There is an appropriate amount of relevant training and development and other forms of learning within the team. Both 'individual' and 'team' learning activities are evident. Once identified, needs are addressed in a timely manner, through quality solutions, the outcomes of which are generally deemed to be successful. A good balance is achieved between developing knowledge, skills and competence. Time is spent in developing the whole team, in particular ensuring that the various members work together effectively.

F: Sound inter-group relations and communications

Relationships and communication channels between this team and other parts of the organisation are very good. The team is generally viewed positively by individuals and departments in other parts of the organisation and, where appropriate, by external customers. There is good evidence of effective working relationships and communications with both individuals and other functional teams and departments.

G: Appropriate management/leadership

The style of leadership and management displayed within the team is likely to be contributing positively towards how motivated and empowered the team are feeling right now. There is a good balance between the amount of support and direction provided to the team. The nature of support and direction is also likely to be good. Communication and feedback between management, individuals and the team as a whole is appropriate in terms of both quality and quantity.

H: Sound team procedures and regular review

Current team processes and procedures are positively contributing towards helping the team to achieve its objectives. Unnecessary or unwieldy processes have been stripped out and/or processes have been appropriately streamlined. The processes are felt to be adding value and there is a sense that they are modified appropriately in response to changing circumstances. The team reviews its work effectively.

J: Output, performance, quality and accountability

Productivity in terms of both quality and quantity is good. 'Input', i.e. work and effort, is balanced by a similar amount of 'output' in terms of desired results. Customer feedback (whether internal or external) is good to excellent. Individuals take responsibility and accept accountability for the achievement of their own objectives and targets, which means that team targets are generally achieved or even exceeded.

K: Morale

There is a strong team spirit and a feeling of 'belonging' within the team. This extends to the whole team, including 'management'. People enjoy working in this team and have fun. Even when the pressure is on, there's a strong team spirit, which helps to keep individual, and team, stress levels lower than they might otherwise be.

L: Empowerment

Team members have the resources they need to enable them to carry out their roles. They feel that they have appropriate freedom to make and implement decisions within the remit of their role. There is a good balance between providing direction/supervision and allowing individuals freedom to act and to genuinely feel empowered. Team members also feel that opportunities exist to contribute towards wider decisions that affect the whole team. The members of this team generally feel well consulted.

M: Change, creativity and challenging the status quo

This is a team that is open to change and continuous improvement. There is a climate of constantly seeking new and better ways of doing things. Completely new ideas often surface, not just refinements or incremental improvements, though of course this also happens. There is a healthy culture of regularly and rigorously challenging the way things are done. The team are aware of, and use, a variety of 'creative thinking tools' and techniques in their discussions and meetings.

N: Decision-making and problem-solving

This team generally makes good decisions. Their decision-making processes are sound and rigorous. There is consultation and involvement of others outside of the immediate team where and when appropriate. Decisions are usually made in a timely manner, which means that issues are usually resolved

quickly. The team are adept at identifying and tackling challenges and obstacles that are likely to get in the way of them
achieving their objectives.

Team performance survey

What?

We are compiling responses from a broad range of companies to find out the key trends in perception of team performance across different industry sectors and sizes of organisations.

Why?

PRIZE DRAW: Complete and submit today to receive the final RESEARCH WHITE PAPER and your chance to win a bottle of champagne.

How?

- It will only take a few minutes of your time. Please answer honestly as all responses will remain anonymous.
- The 13 paragraphs (A–N) below contain statements that correspond to 13 key team performance indicators.
- Fill in your contact details then read each of the 13 paragraphs and score each according to how you perceive your team performance.
- Score between 1 and 10—1 being strong disagreement, and 10 being strong agreement of the paragraph.

Name: _____

Title: _____

Company: _____

Email: _____

Members in team: _____

Employees in company: _____

Industry sector: _____

Read the statements in each paragraph (A–N) then score from 1–10.
1 being strong disagreement of the statements, 10 being strong
agreement

A: Balanced roles   Score

People understand both their own and other team members'
roles. There is flexibility within the team and a preparedness and
ability to help each other. Work is allocated according to
individuals' capabilities and skills. There is a good sense that we
have the right expertise and that we are well balanced as a
working team.

B: Clear objectives and purpose

The team has a well-communicated 'purpose', and objectives are
clearly defined. Team members fully understand their own
objectives and the way in which they can contribute towards
achieving the team's goals. There is a good sense that team
members are all 'pulling in the same direction'. There is a good
balance between time spent on 'doing' and on necessary
'planning'.

C: Openness, trust, confrontation and conflict resolution

Team members are open with, and trust, one another.
Consequently, they are happy to confront any issues that may
arise between them, sharing information and feelings openly.
Consequently, conflicts and disagreements that do arise are
usually resolved successfully.

D: Cooperation, support, interpersonal communication and relationships

Score

Team members cooperate with and support one another, helping each other out when the pressure is on. There is good interpersonal communication and relationships within the team are strong. Listening to one another is a key strength of this team, as is mutual trust between team members. Team members give each other appropriate and useful feedback aimed at improving individual and team performance.

E: Individual and team learning and development

There is an appropriate amount of relevant training and development, and other forms of learning within the team. Both 'individual' and 'team' learning activities are evident. Once identified, needs are addressed in a timely manner, through quality solutions, the outcomes of which are generally deemed to be successful. A good balance is achieved between developing knowledge, skills and competence. Time is spent in developing the whole team, in particular ensuring that the various members work together effectively.

F: Sound inter-group relations and communications

Relationships and communication channels between this team and other parts of the organisation are very good. The team is generally viewed positively by individuals and departments in other parts of the organisation and, where appropriate, by external customers. There is good evidence of effective working relationships and communications with both individuals and other functional teams and departments.

G: Appropriate management/leadership

The style of leadership and management displayed within the team is likely to be contributing positively towards how motivated and empowered the team are feeling right now. There is a good balance between the amount of support and direction provided to the team. The nature of support and direction is also likely to be good. Communication and feedback between management, individuals and the team as a whole is appropriate in terms of both quality and quantity.

Score

H: Sound team procedures and regular review

Current team processes and procedures are positively contributing towards helping the team to achieve its objectives. Unnecessary or unwieldy processes have been stripped out, and/or processes have been appropriately streamlined. The processes are felt to be adding value, and there is a sense that they are modified appropriately in response to changing circumstances. The team reviews its work effectively.

J: Output, performance, quality and accountability

Productivity in terms of both quality and quantity is good. 'Input', i.e. work and effort, is balanced by a similar amount of 'output' in terms of desired results. Customer feedback (whether internal or external) is good to excellent. Individuals take responsibility, and accept accountability for the achievement of their own objectives and targets, which means that team targets are generally achieved or even exceeded.

K: Morale

There is a strong team spirit and a feeling of 'belonging' within the team. This extends to the whole team, including 'management'. People enjoy working in this team and have fun. Even when the pressure is on, there's a strong team spirit which helps to keep individual and team stress levels lower than they might otherwise be.

L: Empowerment

Team members are equipped with the resources necessary to enable them to carry out their role. They also have the freedom

to make and implement decisions within the remit of their role. **Score**
All team members have the opportunity to contribute towards
wider decisions that affect the whole team.

M: Change, creativity and challenging the status quo

This is a team that is open to change and continuous
improvement. There is a climate of constantly seeking new and
better ways of doing things. Completely new ideas are often
surfaced, not just refinements or incremental improvements,
though of course this also happens. There is a healthy culture of
regularly and rigorously challenging the way things are done.
The team are aware of, and use, a variety of 'creative thinking
tools' and techniques in their discussions and meetings.

N: Decision-making and problem-solving

This team generally makes good decisions. Their decision-
making processes are sound and rigorous. There is consultation
and involvement of others outside of the immediate team where
and when appropriate. Decisions are usually made in a timely
manner, which means that issues are usually resolved quickly.
The team are adept at identifying and tackling challenges and
obstacles that are likely to get in the way of them achieving
their objectives.

Comments

Appendix 3
A sample TPD report

What follows is a reproduction of a sample Team Performance Diagnostic (TPD) report produced by SIA Group. Please note that this is a black-and-white reproduction; the actual report is in full colour.

SIA Group

LEADERS IN TRAINING & DEVELOPMENT

TEAM PERFORMANCE Diagnostics

Team Performance Analysis

Team results measured against average results for the whole TPD data base

This report will enable you to:

- Identify areas for team development quickly and accurately

- Target your development budget more effectively or specific issues

- Gain an invaluable insight into the underlying dynamics within your team and to identify very specific areas for development

ABC Technologies Marketing Team

Tel: +44 (0) 1903 812700
Fax: +44 (0) 1903 879142
Web: www.siagroup.co.uk
Email: enquiries@siagroup.co.uk

SIA Group

39 High Street, Steyning
West Sussex, BN44 3YE

Introduction to the SIA Team Performance Diagnostic

Team Performance Diagnostic

Who are SIA?

Our Mission is simple … to 'Inspire Excellence'

Since 1982 we have grown our business through working closely with many organisations to design, develop and deliver exceptional solutions in the following areas:

> Diagnostic Tools to improve Personal and Organisational Performance

> Facilitated Workshops

> Training Programmes

> 1:1 Coaching

> Organisational Development and Team-Building Events

Our aim is to inspire people and enable them to excel.

SIA diagnostic tools are based upon the very latest theories and management thinking in the world of personal and organisational performance, combined with the experience and understanding of what works in practice.

All our work has a practical focus, linking theory to real life and workplace situations. This means that participants find many opportunities to apply what they learn with SIA to their work and their personal lives.

From our base near Brighton, in the South of England, we run programmes throughout the world. We currently have clients in Asia, America, Europe, Africa and the Middle East. As a result, we gain a deep understanding of many diverse cultures and how they operate. This perspective enriches the programmes we deliver to all our clients whether they are from the public or private sector, large or small.

The SIA team of experienced facilitators, trainers and coaches together with our office-based Client Support Team are committed to ensuring the conduct, administration and organisation of all SIA work meets our exceptionally high standards.

Above all, we care about learning and development, your learning and development.

I am confident that this passion for Inspiring Excellence in all our work will come across in all contact you have with SIA.

After all, it's our mission!

George Siantonas

Chairman

Office: 39 High Street, Steyning, West Sussex, BN44 3YE

Tel: +44 (0)1903 812700   Fax: +44 (0)1903 879142

email: info@siagroup.co.uk   Web: www.siagroup.co.uk

SIAGroup

LEADERS IN TRAINING & DEVELOPMENT

Team Performance Diagnostic

Team Performance Diagnostic ©

A Diagnostic Instrument Developed by the SIA Group for building 'Optimum Team Performance'

Introduction

In organisations today teams are responsible for accomplishing many tasks. A team can often achieve much more than the sum of its individual members, yet harnessing this synergy can be a complex process, and it's critical to know where to focus.

This report is based upon the collective responses of members of the Marketing Team team to the 'Team Performance Diagnostic©' tool.

The 'Team Performance Diagnostic©' tool has been carefully designed to pinpoint specific areas of performance improvement within this team. Its comprehensive nature, involving 156 quick and easy to answer questions, covers all critical aspects of team performance.

The information within this report will enable the Marketing Team team to take positive actions in those areas where they are likely to generate the greatest return in terms of team performance improvement.

Format of the Report

The 13 Team Performance Indicators used to measure a team's performance are represented graphically in section 2 in the summary graphs and are labelled A – N.

The higher the column for each Team Performance Indicator the more successful the team is with respect to that specific team performance area.

A 'traffic light system' clearly differentiates the Team Performance Indicator results:

Red	=	Lowest Performance Indicators	=	Priorities for Action
Amber	=	Mid-Range Performance Indicators	=	Focus and Improve
Green	=	Highest Performance Indicators	=	Build and Maintain

Further narrative relating to each of the 13 Team Performance Indicators, and clustered into the 'traffic light system', gives further qualitative details and guidance that helps to pinpoint specifically what's working and what's not.

It is possible to drill still deeper into the analysis to identify those specific components of each of the 13 Team Performance Indicators that are leading to relatively low scores.

By focusing upon the red areas initially, with an eye to the amber, the leader of the team is able to target more clearly development activities in order to redress imbalances, bridge gaps and raise the performance of the team as a whole.

Detailed Analysis

The real power of this tool comes to light when a detailed analysis is performed upon the individual Team Performance Indicators themselves, in particular, focusing attention upon the 'red' and 'amber' areas.

Overleaf, are detailed graphs relating to each of the 13 Team Performance Indicators, which enable us to drill into the specific elements of each.

For example, how team members feel about 'Morale' will be determined by many things such as the level of team spirit, management style, the amount of 'fun' within the team, individual stress levels etc.

Things to watch out for:

The score for each broad Team Performance Indicator is arrived at through a combination of 12 specific, more detailed elements, thus:

> A relatively high (green) Team Performance Indicator may, in fact, have a small number of low scoring elements that are masked at the broader Team Performance Indicator level

> A relatively low scoring (red) Team Performance Indicator may, in fact have some good practices which need to be preserved and built upon. These are masked by the fact that the average score is dragged down by some particularly poor elements

> An average (amber) Team Performance Indicator can appear average when in fact this is arrived at by a combination of both good and poor practices - extremes at both ends that compensate for each other

The key message therefore is that the real benefit of this tool is in focusing attention upon the elements of behaviour, practices, systems and management style etc that go to make up each of the 13 Team Performance Indicators for optimum team performance.

It is from this level of analysis that the most appropriate Action Plan can be built, specifically targeted at those areas that will yield the biggest return in terms of team performance and therefore team results.

Additionally, it is worth remembering that a team is composed of individuals, and hence, whilst the team will have its 'collective profile', this is arrived at through the aggregation of a number of 'individual profiles'. Thus:

> It is quite common within any team to have a small number of individuals who are generally unhappy with the way things are at present, and hence tend to 'drag down' the scores for the whole team

> Equally, there are usually some individuals who are very happy with how things are for them within the team. Their scoring will tend to 'lift up' the scores for the whole team

A further level of analysis is possible to indicate the degree to which this may be happening in your team, whilst retaining anonymity of the source data.

Team Performance Indicators Summary Graphs

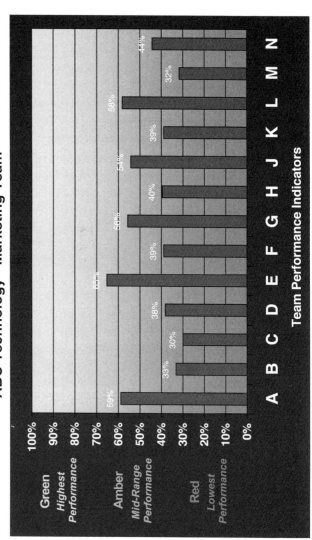

Team Performance Indicators - Summary Graph

Team Perfomance Diagnostic

ABC Technology - Marketing Team

04/08/2006

No. of respondents in team: 12

A. Balanced Roles

B. Clear Objectives and Purpose

C. Openness, trust, confrontation and conflict resolution

D. Co-operation, support, interpersonal communication and relationships

E. Individual and team learning and development

F. Sound inter-group relations and communications

G. Appropriate Management / Leadership

H. Sound team procedures and regular review

J. Output, performance, quality and accountability

K. Morale

L. Empowerment

M. Change, creativity challenge the status quo

N. Decision-making and problem solving

SIA Group
LEADERS IN TRAINING & DEVELOPMENT

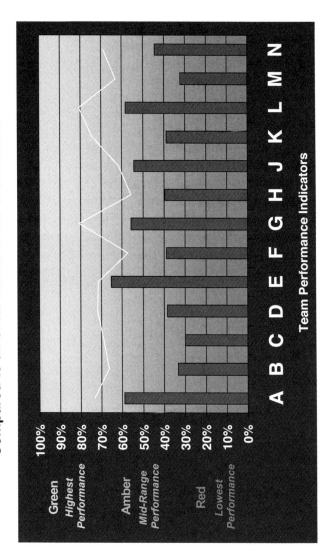

Team Performance Diagnostic

Team Performance Indicators - Summary Graph

ABC Technology - Marketing Team

Compared to all other teams in the TPD Database

04/08/2006

———— **Average of all other teams in the TPD Database**

A. Balanced Roles

B. Clear Objectives and Purpose

C. Openness, trust, confrontation and conflict resolution

D. Co-operation, support, interpersonal communication and relationships

E. Individual and team learning and development

F. Sound inter-group relations and communications

G. Appropriate Management / Leadership

H. Sound team procedures and regular review

J. Output, performance, quality and accountability

K. Morale

L. Empowerment

M. Change, creativity challenge the status quo

N. Decision-making and problem solving

SIA Group
LEADERS IN TRAINING & DEVELOPMENT

Team Performance Diagnostic

Team Performance Indicators - Summary Graph

ABC Technology - Marketing Team

compared to

ABC Technology - Marketing Team Leader

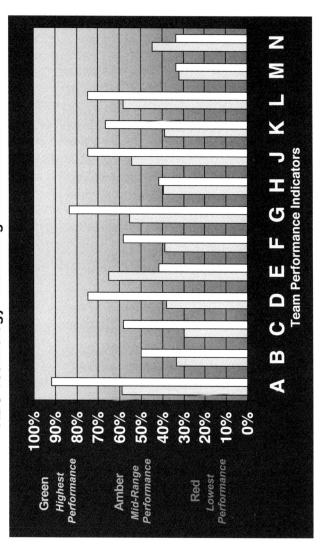

04/08/2006

■ Marketing Team respondents: 12

□ Marketing Team Leader respondents: 1

A. Balanced Roles

B. Clear Objectives and Purpose

C. Openness, trust, confrontation and conflict resolution

D. Co-operation, support, interpersonal communication and relationships

E. Individual and team learning and development

F. Sound inter-group relations and communications

G. Appropriate Management / Leadership

H. Sound team procedures and regular review

J. Output, performance, quality and accountability

K. Morale

L. Empowerment

M. Change, creativity challenge the status quo

N. Decision-making and problem solving

Team Performance Diagnostic

Team Performance Indicators - Summary Graph

ABC Technology - Marketing Team

compared to

ABC Technology - Human Resources Team

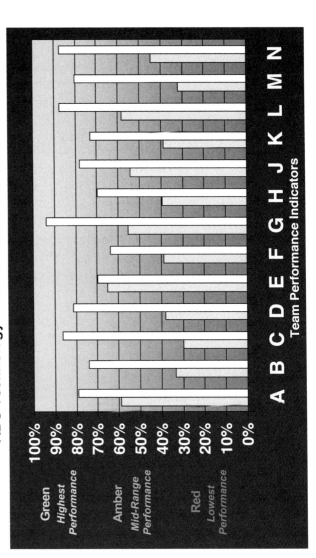

04/08/2006

Marketing Team respondents: 12

Human Resources Team respondents: 8

A. Balanced Roles

B. Clear Objectives and Purpose

C. Openness, trust, confrontation and conflict resolution

D. Co-operation, support, interpersonal communication and relationships

E. Individual and team learning and development

F. Sound inter-group relations and communications

G. Appropriate Management / Leadership

H. Sound team procedures and regular review

J. Output, performance, quality and accountability

K. Morale

L. Empowerment

M. Change, creativity challenge the status quo

N. Decision-making and problem solving

SIAGroup

LEADERS IN TRAINING & DEVELOPMENT

Development Focus

Team Performance Diagnostic

Development Focus

Lowest Performance Indicators

Priorities for Action

The Detailed Analysis section (see later) provides deep insight into which specific elements are contributing to a relatively low Team Performance Score for this team.

The paragraphs below simply give a 'generic' description of the lower scoring Performance Indicators. Hence, some, but probably not all of these guidelines are likely to apply to this team.

Treat this section as an 'indication' of what might be going on rather than fact.

B. Clear Objectives and Purpose

The team's purpose may not be as well-communicated as necessary and/or objectives may need to be more clearly defined. Team members may not fully understand their own objectives and the way in which they can contribute towards achieving the team's goals. There may be some element of team members 'pulling in different directions'. It is possible that far more focus is being placed upon 'doing' rather than 'planning'.

C. Openness, trust, confrontation and conflict resolution

Team members may not fully trust one another. Consequently, there is a tendency to avoid confronting issues that may arise between them in an open and honest way. Sharing of information and feelings between team members may be lower than necessary. Consequently, some conflicts and disagreements tend to remain unresolved.

D. Co-operation, support, interpersonal communication and relationships

Team members may not co-operate with, nor support one another as much as they could. When the pressure is on it may be a case of 'heads down' and get on with your own job. Interpersonal communications and relationships could be improved within the team. Listening to each other and mutual trust between team members could be improved. The evidence indicates that team members may give each other insufficient feedback aimed at improving individual and team performance.

M. Change, creativity challenge the status quo

It may be that the team, or a significant number of individuals within the team, are less open to change than they could be. A climate of stability can lead to the team tending to be 'risk-averse' rather than seeking continuous, active improvement. Completely new ideas may rarely surface. There may be a need to evolve a stronger culture of regularly and rigorously challenging the way things are done to encourage new ways of thinking and to equip the team with powerful 'creative thinking tools'.

Team Performance Diagnostic

Development Focus

Mid-Range Performance Indicators

Focus and Improve

The Detailed Analysis section (see later) provides deep insight into which specific elements are contributing to a mid-range Team Performance Score for this team.

The paragraphs below simply give a 'generic' description of the mid-range scoring Performance Indicators. It is likely that you would want to explore some or all of the following areas in more detail:

F. Sound inter-group relations and communications

How could relationships and communication channels between this team and other parts of the organisation be improved? Are there issues around the image others have of this team, and of how the team is projected to both internal and external customers? In what ways could we work more actively with, and communicate to and from other functions, departments and teams?

H. Sound team procedures and regular review

How appropriate are current procedures and processes in terms of helping the team to achieve its objectives? Could some be seen as bureaucratic, adding little value, and/or not changing over time in response to changing circumstances? In what ways could the team plan and review its work more effectively?

J. Output, performance, quality and accountability

Could the quality of productivity be improved? What about quantity, could there be improvements in this area? How do the team feel about the amount of 'input' in terms of work and effort they expend, and the amount of 'output' as measured in desired results? What does customer feedback (internal and/or external) reveal? Could some team members, or the team as a whole take more responsibility and accountability for the achievement of objectives and targets? Are targets missed more often than not? If so, this may indicate that improvements in this are could be the way forward.

K. Morale

Could the team benefit from a little more 'team spirit'? Do team members feel a real sense of belonging, and have a strong team identity? How integrated are 'management' into the team, or could there be some feeling that management, whilst leaders of the team, are not part of the real 'social' team? Could there be a little more enjoyment and fun within the team? What about when the pressure is on – what happens to team spirit, morale and individual stress levels then?

N. Decision-making and problem solving

How effective are decision-making processes, as judged by the quality of decisions that the team, and individual members, make? Could others be involved more, perhaps at different levels? How about the timing of decisions, could some decisions be made faster and therefore issues resolved sooner? How good is the team at identifying and tackling challenges and obstacles in order to achieve their objectives?

Team Performance Diagnostic

Development Focus

Highest Performance Indicators

Build and Maintain

The Green areas are also revealing, though in a different way, in that they highlight what's working really well in the team.

It is important to recognise what's working well as this enables us to preserve and build upon good practices, whilst at the same time tackling those areas that need corrective action.

Celebrating what we do well in a team is also good for morale and team spirit.

The Detailed Analysis section (see later) will provide insight into which specific elements are contributing to a relatively high Team Performance Score in these broad areas.

As a 'top-line' summary, it is likely that some or all of the following applies:

A. Balanced Roles

People understand both their own and other team members' roles. There is flexibility within the team and a preparedness and ability to help each other. Work is allocated according to individuals' capabilities and skills. There is a good sense that we have the right expertise and that we are well balanced as a working team.

E. Individual and team learning and development

There is an appropriate amount of relevant training and development, and other forms of learning within the team. Both 'individual' and 'team' learning activities are evident. Once identified, needs are addressed in a timely manner, through quality solutions, the outcomes of which are generally deemed to be successful. A good balance is achieved between developing knowledge, skills and competence. Time is spent in developing the whole team, in particular ensuring that the various members work together effectively.

G. Appropriate Management / Leadership

The style of leadership and management displayed within the team is likely to be contributing positively towards how motivated and empowered the team are feeling right now. There is a good balance between the amount of support and direction provided to the team. The nature of support and direction is also likely to be good. Communication, and feedback between management, individuals and the team as a whole is appropriate in terms of both quality and quantity.

L. Empowerment

Team members have the resources they need to enable them to carry out their roles. They feel that they have appropriate freedom to make and implement decisions within the remit of their role. There is a good balance between providing direction/supervision and allowing individuals freedom to act and to genuinely feel empowered. Team members also feel that opportunities exist to contribute towards wider decisions which affect the whole team. The members of this team generally feel well consulted.

Detailed Graphs for each Indicator

SIA Group - Team Performance Diagnostic
ABC Technology - Marketing Team

A. Balanced Roles   59%

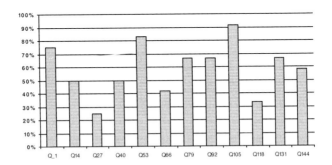

B. Clear Objectives and Purpose   33%

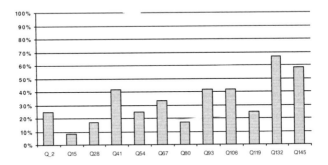

C. Openness, trust, confrontation and conflict resolution   30%

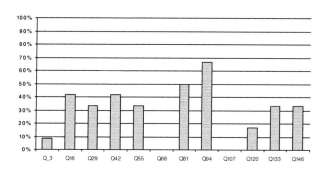

D. Co-operation, support, interpersonal communication and relationships   38%

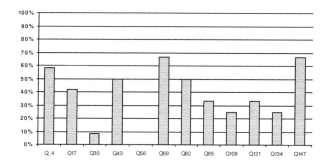

SIA Group - Team Performance Diagnostic
ABC Technology - Marketing Team

E. Individual and team learning and development   65%

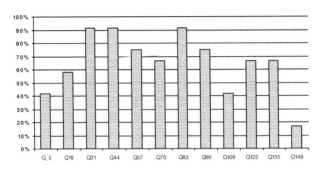

F. Sound inter-group relations and communications   39%

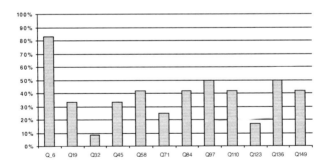

G. Appropriate Management / Leadership   56%

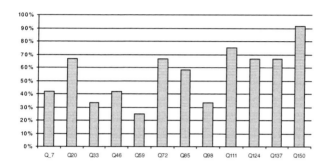

H. Sound team procedures and regular review   40%

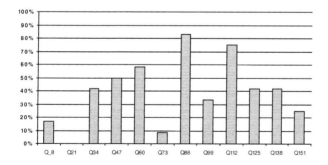

04/08/2006

SIA Group - Team Performance Diagnostic
ABC Technology - Marketing Team

J. Output, performance, quality and accountability   54%

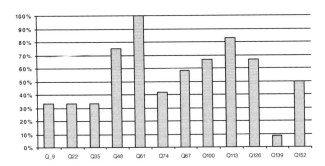

K. Morale   39%

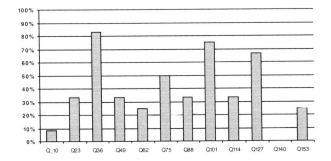

L. Empowerment   58%

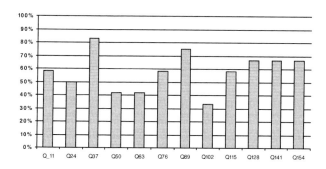

M. Change, creativity challenge the status quo   32%

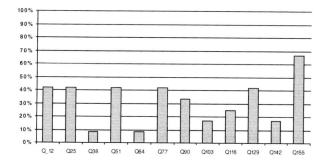

SIA Group - Team Performance Diagnostic
ABC Technology - Marketing Team

N. Decision-making and problem solving   44%

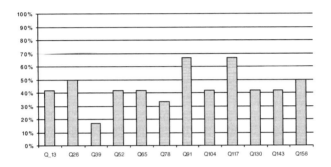

Detailed Tables for each Indicator

SIA Group - Team Performance Diagnostic
ABC Technology - Marketing Team
Data Tables

A. Balanced Roles   59%

1. We often find that we lack the required expertise.	14. There should be more flexibility in my job content	27. We do not utilise the skills we have available sufficiently.	40. It's sometimes difficult to help out team members as our jobs seem to be so different.	53. We have too many specialists in our team.	66. When a key person is away then work tends to pile up in that area or cause a bottleneck.
Y	Y	Y	N	N	N
N	N	Y	Y	Y	Y
Y	Y	Y	N	N	Y
Y	Y	Y	Y	N	Y
N	N	N	N	N	N
N	N	Y	Y	N	Y
N	Y	Y	Y	Y	Y
N	N	N	N	N	N
N	Y	N	Y	N	N
N	N	Y	N	N	N
N	N	Y	Y	N	Y
N	Y	Y	N	N	Y

No	75%	50%	25%	50%	83%	42%

A low score is indicative of potential issues and may be worth further consideration

SIA Group
LEADERS IN TRAINING & DEVELOPMENT

79. Too much time is spent defining territory, roles, boundaries and responsibilities.	92. There are some key competencies missing from our team.	105. We have too many people with similar skills.	118. Our team seems to be out of 'balance' in terms of roles.	131. Team members are not prepared to help out when it it's not part of their job.	144. I have no clear idea of what other team members are doing.
N	Y	N	Y	Y	N
Y	N	N	N	N	N
N	N	Y	Y	N	Y
Y	Y	N	Y	Y	N
N	N	N	N	N	N
N	N	N	Y	N	Y
N	N	N	Y	N	Y
Y	N	N	N	N	N
Y	N	N	N	N	N
N	N	N	Y	N	N
N	Y	N	Y	Y	Y
N	Y	N	Y	Y	Y
67%	**67%**	**92%**	**33%**	**67%**	**58%**

N=No/Disagree, Y=Yes/Agree

04/08/2006

SIA Group - Team Performance Diagnostic
ABC Technology - Marketing Team
Data Tables

B. Clear Objectives and Purpose   33%

2. No-one is really clear where we are going.	15. We are all very busy but we don't seem to be pulling in the same direction.	28. We do not spend enough time planning for the future.	41. We do not have a clear view of what is expected of us.	54. Longer term planning meetings don't happen enough.	67. The goalposts keep moving.
Y	Y	Y	Y	Y	N
Y	Y	N	Y	Y	Y
Y	Y	Y	Y	Y	Y
Y	Y	Y	Y	Y	Y
N	Y	Y	N	N	Y
Y	Y	Y	Y	Y	N
Y	Y	Y	N	Y	N
N	Y	Y	N	N	Y
N	N	N	N	N	Y
Y	Y	Y	N	Y	N
Y	Y	Y	Y	Y	Y
Y	Y	Y	Y	Y	Y

No	25%	8%	17%	42%	25%	33%

A low score is indicative of potential issues and may be worth further consideration

SIA Group
LEADERS IN TRAINING & DEVELOPMENT

80. Sometimes it feels as though we're going round in circles without getting anywhere.	93. Our Team is not sufficiently results orientated.	106. Planning meetings tend to leave me even more confused than before we started.	119. Our team's priorities are unclear.	132. I do not know exactly what my objectives are.	145. I do not understand how my own objectives relate to those of the team.
Y	Y	Y	Y	Y	Y
Y	N	N	Y	N	N
Y	N	Y	Y	Y	Y
Y	Y	Y	Y	Y	Y
N	N	N	N	N	N
Y	Y	Y	Y	N	N
Y	Y	Y	N	N	N
Y	N	N	N	N	N
N	N	N	Y	N	N
Y	Y	N	Y	N	N
Y	Y	Y	Y	Y	Y
Y	Y	Y	Y	N	Y
17%	**42%**	**42%**	**25%**	**67%**	**58%**

N=No/Disagree, Y=Yes/Agree

04/08/2006

SIA Group - Team Performance Diagnostic
ABC Technology - Marketing Team
Data Tables

C. Openness, trust, confrontation and conflict resolution   30%

3. People do not tend to say what they really think or feel.	16. Conflict is often destructive in this team.	29. It would help if people were more willing to admit their mistakes.	42. We are not as honest with each other as we should or could be.	55. It is the strong personalities in the team that tend to get their own way.	68. Conflicts and disagreements which should really be flushed out tend to be avoided.
Y	Y	Y	Y	Y	Y
Y	N	Y	N	N	Y
Y	Y	Y	Y	Y	Y
Y	Y	Y	Y	Y	Y
Y	N	N	N	N	Y
Y	Y	N	Y	Y	Y
Y	Y	Y	Y	Y	Y
N	N	N	N	Y	Y
Y	N	Y	N	Y	Y
Y	N	N	N	N	Y
Y	Y	Y	Y	Y	Y
Y	Y	Y	Y	N	Y

No	8%	42%	33%	42%	33%	0%

A low score is indicative of potential issues and may be worth further consideration

81. Some people within our team back down too easily when challenged.	94. There is a sense of hostility among parts of this team.	107. Delicate issues are not raised within the team - issues are often brushed under the carpet.	120. More time should be devoted to discussing and valuing our differences within the team.	133. People are afraid to raise controversial issues within the team.	146. Team, members often work to their own 'hidden' agendas.
N	Y	Y	Y	Y	Y
N	N	Y	N	Y	N
N	Y	Y	Y	Y	Y
Y	Y	Y	Y	Y	Y
Y	N	Y	N	N	N
Y	N	Y	Y	Y	Y
Y	N	Y	Y	Y	Y
N	N	Y	Y	N	Y
N	N	Y	Y	N	N
Y	N	Y	Y	N	N
Y	Y	Y	Y	Y	Y
N	N	Y	Y	Y	Y
50%	67%	0%	17%	33%	33%

N=No/Disagree, Y=Yes/Agree

04/08/2006

SIA Group - Team Performance Diagnostic
ABC Technology - Marketing Team

Data Tables

D. Co-operation, support, interpersonal communication and

4. When the going gets tough it tends to be everyone for him/herself.	17. There is little loyalty between members of the team.	30. We do not really work together - individuals tend to get on with their own work.	43. I do not receive sufficient feedback from other team members.	56. We do not pay sufficient attention to relationships within the team.	69. I do not feel supported by my colleagues.
Y	Y	Y	Y	Y	N
Y	N	Y	N	Y	N
Y	Y	Y	Y	Y	Y
Y	Y	Y	Y	Y	Y
N	N	Y	N	Y	N
N	Y	Y	Y	Y	N
Y	Y	Y	Y	Y	Y
N	N	Y	N	Y	Y
N	N	N	N	Y	N
N	N	Y	N	Y	N
N	Y	Y	N	Y	N
N	Y	Y	Y	Y	N
No 58%	42%	8%	50%	0%	67%

A low score is indicative of potential issues and may be worth further consideration

relationships   38%

82. There are too many recriminations between team members.	95. There is not enough listening going on within our team.	108. Trust is generally low between team members.	121. People seem unwilling to take the views of others into account quite a lot of the time.	134. We could really do with some help on how to improve our own team communications.	147. I do not feel trusted.
Y	Y	Y	Y	Y	Y
N	N	N	Y	N	N
Y	Y	Y	Y	Y	Y
Y	Y	Y	Y	Y	Y
N	N	N	N	N	N
N	Y	Y	N	Y	Y
N	Y	Y	Y	Y	N
Y	N	N	N	Y	N
N	Y	Y	Y	Y	N
N	N	Y	N	N	N
Y	Y	Y	Y	Y	N
Y	Y	Y	Y	Y	N
50%	**33%**	**25%**	**33%**	**25%**	**67%**

N=No/Disagree, Y=Yes/Agree

04/08/2006

SIA Group - Team Performance Diagnostic
ABC Technology - Marketing Team
Data Tables

E. Individual and team learning and development   65%

5. Insufficient learning and development opportunities are created within the work we do.	18. Often, the wrong kinds of skills are developed within our team.	31. When I've asked for training it either doesn't happen, or takes an age before it gets organised.	44. Our team's manager does not take my personal development seriously enough.	57. Individuals are not encouraged to grow, professionally and/or personally.	70. Our manager does not have sufficient skills to develop others.
Y	Y	N	N	N	Y
N	N	N	N	N	N
Y	Y	Y	Y	Y	Y
Y	Y	N	N	Y	Y
N	N	N	N	N	N
N	N	N	N	N	N
Y	N	N	N	N	N
N	N	N	N	N	N
Y	N	N	N	N	N
N	N	N	N	N	N
Y	Y	N	N	N	N
Y	Y	N	N	Y	Y
No 42%	58%	92%	92%	75%	67%

A low score is indicative of potential issues and may be worth further consideration

SIA Group
LEADERS IN TRAINING & DEVELOPMENT

83.The subject of 'training' comes up periodically, but nothing really seems to materialise.	96. We should spend more time developing our own people rather than recruiting externally.	109. I don't feel stretched or particularly challenged in my role.	122. People are not really helped to develop.	135. Personal development tends to be something that you do yourself and in your own time.	148. We rarely spend time/money on team building and team development.
N	Y	Y	N	Y	Y
N	N	N	N	N	Y
Y	Y	Y	Y	Y	Y
N	N	Y	Y	Y	Y
N	N	N	N	N	Y
N	N	Y	N	N	Y
N	N	Y	N	N	Y
N	Y	N	N	N	N
N	N	N	Y	N	Y
N	N	N	N	Y	Y
N	N	Y	N	N	Y
N	N	Y	Y	N	N
92%	**75%**	**42%**	**67%**	**67%**	**17%**

N=No/Disagree, Y=Yes/Agree

04/08/2006

SIA Group - Team Performance Diagnostic
ABC Technology - Marketing Team
Data Tables

F. Sound inter-group relations and communications   39%

6. We are often in conflict with other departments.	19. Relationships with other groups and departments tend to be distant and rather cool.	32. We don't project our position or raise our profile well enough within the broader organisation.	45. We do not seek sufficient feedback on this team from others outside the team.	58. There is little help or co-operation between our team and other teams in the organisation.	71. It's a bit of a 'closed shop' here - we tend to keep ourselves to ourselves.
N	Y	Y	Y	Y	Y
N	Y	Y	N	N	Y
Y	Y	Y	Y	Y	Y
N	Y	Y	Y	Y	Y
N	N	N	N	N	N
N	Y	Y	Y	Y	Y
N	Y	Y	Y	Y	Y
N	N	Y	N	N	N
N	N	Y	N	N	N
N	N	Y	Y	Y	Y
Y	Y	Y	Y	N	Y
N	Y	Y	Y	Y	Y

No	83%	33%	8%	33%	42%	25%

A low score is indicative of potential issues and may be worth further consideration

84. We are not very good at listening to our internal or external customers.	97. We do not really understand what other departments are trying to achieve.	110. There's little evidence of us working closely with other teams.	123. We have too little influence on the rest of the organisation.	136. We do not proactively reach out to help other groups and teams.	149. Information does not flow freely enough between our team and other teams.
Y	N	Y	Y	Y	Y
Y	Y	N	Y	N	N
Y	Y	N	Y	N	Y
Y	Y	Y	Y	Y	Y
N	N	N	N	N	N
Y	N	Y	Y	Y	N
Y	N	Y	Y	Y	Y
N	N	N	N	N	N
N	N	N	Y	N	Y
N	Y	Y	Y	N	N
N	Y	Y	Y	Y	Y
Y	Y	Y	Y	Y	Y
42%	**50%**	**42%**	**17%**	**50%**	**42%**

N=No/Disagree, Y=Yes/Agree

04/08/2006

SIA Group - Team Performance Diagnostic
ABC Technology - Marketing Team
Data Tables

G. Appropriate Management / Leadership 56%

7. We do not get enough feedback from our manager.	20. Our manager is not always always true to their word.	33. Our manager sometimes does not demonstrate their support for the team when dealing with others.	46. The way an individual is valued within the team has little to do with what they achieve.	59. I lack confidence in the way in which our team is led and managed.	72. Our manager takes little interest in team members until something goes wrong.
Y	Y	Y	Y	Y	Y
N	Y	Y	N	Y	N
Y	Y	Y	Y	Y	Y
Y	Y	Y	Y	Y	Y
N	N	N	N	N	N
Y	N	Y	Y	Y	Y
Y	N	Y	Y	Y	N
N	N	N	N	N	N
N	N	N	N	N	N
N	N	N	N	Y	N
Y	N	Y	Y	Y	N
Y	N	Y	Y	Y	N

No	42%	67%	33%	42%	25%	67%

A low score is indicative of potential issues and may be worth further consideration

85. I do not feel that we always get 'full and honest' feedback from our manager.	98. Our manager does not make the best use of us, either individually or as a team.	111. Useful contributions and successes are not sufficiently recognised by the manager of the team.	124. My manager rarely seems to have the time to listen to my problems and issues.	137. My manager often gives me instructions on how to do things I can already do.	150. I often find myself struggling with new tasks with little or no guidance.
Y	Y	Y	Y	Y	N
N	Y	Y	N	N	N
Y	Y	N	Y	Y	N
Y	Y	Y	N	Y	Y
N	N	N	N	N	N
Y	Y	N	Y	N	N
N	Y	N	Y	N	N
N	N	N	N	Y	N
N	N	N	N	N	N
N	N	N	N	N	N
N	Y	N	N	N	N
Y	Y	N	N	N	N
58%	**33%**	**75%**	**67%**	**67%**	**92%**

N=No/Disagree, Y=Yes/Agree

04/08/2006

SIA Group - Team Performance Diagnostic
ABC Technology - Marketing Team
Data Tables

H. Sound team procedures and regular review   40%

8. Internal communication channels, between members of our own team, need improving.	21. We do not review or analyse the usefulness of our meetings often enough.	34. Often the information I need to do my job properly is inadequate.	47. We do not seem to learn from our mistakes, often blundering on without reviewing properly.	60. Information is not shared sufficiently within the team.	73. We should spend more time questioning the way we operate.
Y	Y	N	Y	N	Y
N	Y	N	N	N	Y
Y	Y	Y	Y	Y	Y
Y	Y	Y	Y	Y	Y
N	Y	N	N	N	N
Y	Y	N	N	N	Y
Y	Y	N	N	Y	Y
Y	Y	Y	N	N	Y
Y	Y	Y	N	Y	Y
Y	Y	Y	Y	N	Y
Y	Y	Y	Y	N	Y
Y	Y	Y	Y	Y	Y

No	17%	0%	42%	50%	58%	8%

A low score is indicative of potential issues and may be worth further consideration

86. We often reach decisions far too quickly.	99. We spend too much time doing and not enough time thinking.	112. We seldom review our working procedures or organisation.	125. The 'left hand' does not know what the 'right hand' is doing.	138. Too few of our good ideas are implemented.	151. It can be difficult to get things done because of all the forms and processes that need to be adhered to.
N	N	Y	Y	Y	Y
N	Y	N	Y	Y	Y
Y	Y	Y	Y	Y	Y
Y	Y	Y	Y	Y	Y
N	N	N	N	N	Y
N	Y	N	N	N	N
N	Y	N	Y	N	Y
N	Y	N	N	Y	Y
N	N	N	N	N	Y
N	N	N	N	N	N
N	Y	N	Y	Y	N
N	Y	N	Y	Y	Y
83%	**33%**	**75%**	**42%**	**42%**	**25%**

N=No/Disagree, Y=Yes/Agree

04/08/2006

SIA Group - Team Performance Diagnostic
ABC Technology - Marketing Team
Data Tables

J. Output, performance, quality and accountability   54%

9. Sometimes I worry about the real quality of our work.	22. We are all working very hard but we don't seem to get very far.	35. There doesn't seem to be enough emphasis on hitting our team objectives.	48. We often fail to achieve our targets.	61. Whilst we may be spending our budget, we are not managing to achieve all of the things we need to do.	74. We usually manage to get the job done, but sometimes it's a bit of a last minute rush.
Y	Y	Y	Y	N	Y
Y	Y	N	N	N	Y
Y	Y	Y	N	N	Y
Y	Y	Y	Y	N	Y
N	N	N	N	N	N
Y	Y	Y	N	N	Y
N	N	Y	N	N	N
Y	Y	Y	N	N	Y
N	N	N	N	N	N
N	N	Y	N	N	N
Y	Y	Y	Y	N	Y
Y	Y	N	N	N	N
No					
33%	33%	33%	75%	100%	42%

A low score is indicative of potential issues and may be worth further consideration

87. There's too much waste in this department.	100. Accountability, blame and credit often get apportioned according to who is popular and who is not.	113. When things are falling behind there doesn't seem to be much of a drive for performance.	126. There are too many complaints from 'customers' (internal/external).	139. I feel that we could achieve much more as a team.	152. Feedback from our customers rarely tells us we are excellent.
Y	Y	Y	Y	Y	Y
N	N	N	N	Y	N
Y	Y	N	Y	Y	Y
Y	Y	Y	N	Y	Y
N	N	N	N	N	N
N	N	N	N	Y	N
N	N	N	N	Y	Y
N	N	N	N	Y	N
N	N	N	N	Y	N
N	N	N	N	Y	N
Y	N	N	Y	Y	Y
Y	Y	N	Y	Y	Y
58%	**67%**	**83%**	**67%**	**8%**	**50%**

N=No/Disagree, Y=Yes/Agree

04/08/2006

SIA Group - Team Performance Diagnostic
ABC Technology - Marketing Team
Data Tables

K. Morale　39%

10. Team spirit is quite low right now.	23. It's not much fun working in this team.	36. When our manager comes around you can sense the dampening effect on the team.	49. I regularly get that Sunday evening 'back to work blues' feeling.	62. We used to have a good laugh working here, now it's all a bit too serious.	75. The 'management' style doesn't exactly promote or boost morale.
Y	Y	Y	Y	Y	Y
Y	Y	N	Y	Y	N
Y	Y	Y	Y	Y	Y
Y	Y	N	Y	Y	Y
Y	N	N	N	N	N
Y	Y	N	Y	Y	Y
Y	Y	N	Y	Y	Y
Y	N	N	Y	Y	N
N	N	N	N	Y	N
Y	N	N	N	N	N
Y	Y	N	N	N	N
Y	Y	N	Y	Y	Y

No	8%	33%	83%	33%	25%	50%

A low score is indicative of potential issues and may be worth further consideration

88. I am quite stressed at the moment.	101. We have too high a turnover of staff within the team.	114. I'm thinking about looking for a new role either inside or outside this organisation.	127. I am sure some team members would rather phone in sick than come in when feeling slightly unwell.	140. We are more like a collection of individuals than a team.	153. There are cliques that have developed within the team that exclude 'non-members'.
Y	Y	Y	Y	Y	Y
N	N	N	N	Y	N
Y	N	Y	Y	Y	Y
Y	N	Y	N	Y	Y
Y	N	N	N	Y	N
Y	Y	Y	N	Y	Y
Y	N	Y	Y	Y	Y
Y	N	Y	N	Y	Y
N	N	N	N	Y	Y
N	Y	N	N	Y	N
N	N	Y	N	Y	Y
Y	N	Y	Y	Y	Y
33%	**75%**	**33%**	**67%**	**0%**	**25%**

N=No/Disagree, Y=Yes/Agree

04/08/2006

SIA Group - Team Performance Diagnostic
ABC Technology - Marketing Team
Data Tables

L. Empowerment   58%

11. Our manager seems unable to trust us to make decisions on our own.	24. In this team it pays to keep your mouth shut.	37. There are too many rules and regulations in our team - it's not healthy nor productive.	50. Command and control would be a good way of describing how things are run around here.	63. I feel quite disempowered.	76. Our manager believes that tighter supervision improves results.
Y	Y	Y	Y	Y	Y
Y	N	N	Y	Y	N
Y	Y	N	Y	Y	Y
Y	Y	Y	Y	Y	Y
N	N	N	N	N	N
N	Y	N	Y	Y	N
N	Y	N	N	N	N
N	N	N	N	N	N
N	N	N	Y	Y	N
N	N	N	N	N	N
N	Y	N	Y	N	Y
Y	N	N	N	Y	Y

No	58%	50%	83%	42%	42%	58%

A low score is indicative of potential issues and may be worth further consideration

89. Our manager makes all the decisions around here.	102. Team members often feel frustrated because they are not consulted.	115. Resources are too tightly controlled by those in authority.	128. Once a decision has been made, our manager will 'stand over us' while we carry out the task.	141. Mistakes are rarely tolerated within this team.	154. Our manager often seems reluctant to delegate.
Y	Y	Y	Y	Y	Y
N	Y	Y	N	Y	N
Y	Y	Y	N	Y	Y
Y	Y	N	Y	Y	Y
N	Y	N	N	N	N
N	Y	N	N	N	N
N	N	N	N	N	N
N	N	Y	Y	N	N
N	N	N	Y	N	N
N	N	N	N	N	N
N	Y	N	N	N	N
N	Y	Y	N	N	Y
75%	**33%**	**58%**	**67%**	**67%**	**67%**

N=No/Disagree, Y=Yes/Agree

04/08/2006

SIA Group - Team Performance Diagnostic
ABC Technology - Marketing Team

Data Tables

M. Change, creativity challenge the status quo   32%

12. Inside this team the status quo is rarely challenged.	25. When things go wrong, there are often recriminations from above.	38. We don't seem to actively use many 'creative thinking tools or techniques' in our discussions and meetings.	51. There are too many taboos in this team - things we should and shouldn't do.	64. We are too risk averse as a team, we tend to choose the safer options.	77. We do not pay sufficient attention to new ideas when they are voiced within the team.
Y	Y	Y	Y	Y	Y
Y	N	Y	N	Y	N
Y	Y	Y	Y	Y	N
Y	Y	Y	Y	Y	Y
N	N	N	N	N	N
Y	N	Y	Y	Y	Y
N	Y	Y	Y	Y	Y
N	Y	Y	N	Y	N
N	N	Y	Y	Y	N
N	N	Y	N	Y	Y
Y	Y	Y	N	Y	Y
Y	Y	Y	Y	Y	Y

No	42%	42%	8%	42%	8%	42%

A low score is indicative of potential issues and may be worth further consideration

90. We do not spend enough time considering alternative solutions.	103. There does not seem to be any process for actively seeking and generating ideas.	116. Ideas from outside the team are not really asked for, and rarely used.	129. Team members are afraid of making mistakes.	142. Some team members are resistant to change.	155. This team's attitude could be described as "If things are OK let's leave them as they are".
Y	Y	Y	Y	Y	Y
Y	Y	Y	Y	Y	N
Y	Y	Y	N	Y	Y
Y	Y	Y	Y	Y	Y
N	N	N	N	N	N
Y	Y	Y	Y	Y	N
N	Y	Y	Y	Y	N
N	N	N	N	Y	N
N	Y	N	N	N	N
Y	Y	Y	N	Y	N
Y	Y	Y	Y	Y	Y
Y	Y	Y	Y	Y	N
33%	17%	25%	42%	17%	67%

N=No/Disagree, Y=Yes/Agree

04/08/2006

SIA Group - Team Performance Diagnostic
ABC Technology - Marketing Team
Data Tables

N. Decision-making and problem solving   44%

13. Inside this team decisions about things seem to be 'announced' - we are rarely consulted.	26. Decisions are taken at the wrong level, often by inappropriate people.	39. We rarely work together to share ideas on the best ways to solve problems.	52. After decisions have been made, the active commitment of team members is often variable.	65. I'm not clear just how decisions are made around here.	78. We seem to go round and round in circles before making a decision.
Y	Y	Y	Y	Y	Y
N	Y	Y	N	N	N
Y	Y	Y	Y	Y	Y
Y	Y	Y	Y	Y	Y
N	N	N	N	N	N
Y	N	Y	N	Y	Y
N	N	Y	N	N	Y
N	N	N	Y	N	Y
Y	N	Y	Y	Y	N
N	N	Y	Y	N	N
Y	Y	Y	N	Y	Y
Y	Y	Y	Y	Y	Y
No 42%	50%	17%	42%	42%	33%

A low score is indicative of potential issues and may be worth further consideration

91. Problem solving is more about blame and punishment rather than a genuine desire to solve things and learn from mistakes.	104. Members of the team are not involved sufficiently in decision-making.	117. We seem to make more bad decisions than good ones.	130. Problems tend to reoccur because they haven't been thoroughly examined and dealt with in the first place.	143. Problems tend to be passed about like hot potatoes with no one owning or attempting to resolve them.	156. Decisions are often made in a rush at the last minute.
Y	Y	Y	Y	Y	Y
N	Y	N	Y	Y	N
Y	Y	Y	Y	Y	Y
Y	Y	Y	Y	Y	Y
N	N	N	N	N	N
N	Y	N	Y	Y	Y
N	N	N	N	N	N
N	N	N	N	N	N
N	N	N	N	N	N
N	N	N	N	N	N
Y	Y	N	Y	Y	Y
N	Y	Y	Y	Y	Y
67%	42%	67%	42%	42%	50%

N=No/Disagree, Y=Yes/Agree

04/08/2006

About the authors

Allam Ahmed

Allam holds a PhD in Economics and Management with backgrounds in Marketing, Strategy and International Business. He is a Full Member and Chartered Marketer of the Chartered Institute of Marketing, UK. He is currently the Director of MSc International Management, University of Sussex (UK) and has substantial experience in research and teaching in Europe, the Middle East and Africa (Belgium, Scotland, Sudan, Saudi Arabia, among others). Allam is editor and author of more than 100 refereed texts and articles in a number of international journals, books, conference proceedings, working papers, etc. He is Founding Editor of the World Review of Entrepreneurship, Management and Sustainable Development (WREMSD), and serves on the editorial board of five international journals in business and management. Allam is the Founding President of World Association for Sustainable Development (WASD) and Expert Advisor to the European Commission on International Scientific Cooperation and the United Nations. He has won several international awards and medals for contribution to international business/management research, including the Royal Agricultural College (UK) Scholarship and Prestigious Book Prize for Best MSc/MBA Dissertation.

George Siantonas

George set up SIA Group in 1982, a business that has now grown into a thriving management consultancy, serving the needs of a diverse range of clients on a global basis. As well as being the CEO of SIA, he is a Senior Principal Consultant. He has led seminars and workshops and advised global clients extensively in management and leadership development. His work has encompassed many countries and regions throughout the world, including Sweden, the Netherlands, Belgium, Italy, Greece, Turkey, Ireland, the UK, the Middle East, North Africa and Asia. As a result, he has gained a deep understanding of many diverse cultures and how they operate. George has a BA in Economics and Philosophy from the University of East Anglia, and has conducted seminars as an Associate Lecturer on the Business Studies degree course at the University of Sussex.

Nicholas Siantonas

Nick is a graduate from Sheffield University, UK, where he gained a BA Hons. in Politics and Economics. He is now works in a global think-tank on future social and business trends. As a consultant with SIA Group, Nick worked extensively on a project to gather research data on the challenges faced by team leaders and team members in 21st-century organisations. He then worked on the statistical analysis of the data and in drawing up the conclusions based on the data analysis, which led to the publication of a White Paper detailing the key findings of the research project that led to the current study.